Advance Praise for *As Professors Lay Dying*

"This is more than a piece of high-quality observation. Beneath the droll vignettes runs an earnest faith we absolutely must sustain: liberal education and the teachers who prevail are crucial to civil society and enlightened culture. If we allow the noble practice of teaching to deteriorate, Berlinerblau rightly insists, we jeopardize all the other things we hold dear."

—Mark Bauerlein,
Author of *The Dumbest Generation*

"[A] passionate, important jeremiad.... Berlinerblau writes eloquently about the goal of 'thoughtfulness' as the quality that good teachers most want to encourage in their students."

—Kim Phillips-Fein, *The New York Times*

"Berlinerblau's book often reads like a comic campus novel."

—Jonathan Marks, Commentary

"With remarkable clarity, the book has articulated how professors feel separated from the mainstream, rather than being integral to it.... His book therefore is narrated with hard-earned wisdom and he has alerted the world of academics on flaws which need to be addressed in the realms of higher education."

—The Statesman

"Whether you are just beginning the college search or are already well on your way to completing your bachelor's degree—or are a parent of such a student—read Campus Confidential. You will be more informed about what actually goes on in college teaching and counseled on how to seek out really good professors. Teaching is only one component of a college education, albeit an indispensable one."

—Dennis Bogusz, *Lire, Ecrire, Penser*

AS PROFESSORS LAY DYING

AS PROFESSORS LAY DYING

SELECTING A COLLEGE AMIDST AN EDUCATIONAL CRISIS

JACQUES BERLINERBLAU

Post Hill
PRESS

A POST HILL PRESS BOOK
ISBN: 979-8-89565-360-9
ISBN (eBook): 979-8-89565-361-6

As Professors Lay Dying:
Selecting a College Amidst an Educational Crisis
© 2025 by Jacques Berlinerblau
All Rights Reserved

Cover design by Conroy Accord

Post Hill
PRESS

Post Hill Press
New York • Nashville
posthillpress.com

Published in the United States of America
1 2 3 4 5 6 7 8 9 10

For Ippolita

"[I]t's true that Molière was working in comedy, and the same problem always arises: you always end up crashing into the same difficulty, which is that life, fundamentally, *is not* comical."

Michel Houellebecq, *The Possibility of an Island*

CONTENTS

PREFACE TO THE SECOND EDITION
AS PROFESSORS LAY DYING

I no longer advise my students to pursue a doctorate in the liberal arts and become a professor just like me. That's a pretty effortless moral flex on my part because not one of them has ever expressed an interest in pursuing a doctorate. Even fewer want to be anything like me.

I totally get where they're coming from. Why any American would clamber up the Alp that leads to becoming a credentialed scholar is beyond my comprehension. Graduate students currently scaling these heights arouse not my sentimentality, but my suspicions. When I chance upon an apprentice art historian, or cultural sociologist, I usually assume they are:

a) The son, daughter, or gender-fluid scion of a meme-coin billionaire
b) Someone whose grip on reality is tenuous
c) A perv trawling the Quad for ass
d) a, b, and probably c

I wrote the book that you are about to read during Donald J. Trump's first presidency, a little less than ten years ago. Back in 2017, I still held out hope that we professors could fix our problem. Our problem was the steady disappearance of tenure-track jobs amid an academic labor force being reduced to poverty. Tenure, I'd be the first to admit, is a peculiar and flawed institution. The first edition of this book, entitled *Campus Confidential: How College Works, and Doesn't, for Professors, Parents and Students*, spent a good deal of time trying to explain the tenure system to puzzled laypersons.

I certainly didn't ignore tenure's flaws, nor was I uncritical of professors. So much so that during a media hit for this book one interviewer quipped, "I take it you're not the most popular guy in the faculty lounge."

"Correct," I responded. "But then again," I continued, "faculty lounges don't exist anymore."

I always thought that was a most instructive exchange.

Although I was critical of my colleagues, I was—and remain—convinced that if tenure undergoes its anticipated extinction event (which I and others have been predicting for years), there will be catastrophic ripple effects.[1] Without tenure there can be no academic freedom. And without academic freedom, a whole set of outcomes with lethal implications for our democracy ensue. How would a scholar whose research exposes the corruption of memecoin billionaires ever remain employed if tenure did not exist?

Call this the "Jane Stanford Scenario." In 1900, before there was tenure, Ms. Stanford (yes, of that Stanford) had no qualms about sacking an economist on the faculty who criticized railroad magnates (like the Stanfords).[2] This reminds us that without tenure, the wealthy and powerful can and will silence *every last critical voice.* I would be remiss, however, if I didn't mention that the martyred professor in question, Edwin A. Ross, was a eugenicist and an anti-Asian loon.[3] This reminds me to state one of the core lessons of this book: everything that happens on campus is a lot more complicated than it initially seems and is kind of, grimly, funny.

Anyhow, tenure's slow demise is often seen as "our" (i.e., the professors') problem, and it certainly is. But I've always felt that it's *your* problem too—and by "you" I mean those who are springing for undergraduate tuition. What you—mom, dad, gramma, anonymous benefactor, whoever—are paying for, especially at elite colleges, is bad and indifferent college teaching.

My thesis is that there is a causal link between the professoriate's misery and the poor product we deliver in the classroom. So, when I talk about how to choose a college, I try to demonstrate how the suffering of scholars impacts the kid sitting in the lecture hall. I'll often function as something of a sommelier of the professoriate, albeit one very eager to direct your attention to the bad vintages, the bottles born of floods and nuclear fallout.

When I first published this book, I still believed that we, the professors, could course correct. We could restore the tenure system *and* renew our commitment to educating our students well. We could, at the very least, give it "the old college try." I used my winged words to rally my colleagues like a linebacker delivering an emotional pregame speech: "JOB SECURITY AND PEDAGOGY ON 3. 1-2-3!"

The Extinction Event

Now, during Donald Trump's second presidency, I no longer deliver motivational speeches. The new title of this second edition, *As Professors Lay Dying*, aptly sums up why I think pep talks are of no use. Do morticians encourage their cadavers to "stay positive"?

I want to stress, however, that the looming annihilation of the professoriate is not mainly the forty-fifth and forty-seventh president's doing, or that of the Republican Party, which he has cast in his own image. Don't get me wrong: the GOP has certainly been doing its best to immiserate professors. In 2021, JD Vance dubbed higher education "the enemy." He continued that "we have to honestly and aggressively attack the universities in this country." That is exactly what we are seeing today—minus the honesty.[4] When The End arrives, the MAGA movement will board its monster trucks, flag-bearing trikes and tricked out Teslas and take a victory lap. The unspeakable truth, however, is that *our wounds are largely self-inflicted*.

Before I get to that, permit me to bring you up to speed on some statistics I cited in the first edition. These will help you grasp why I am so pessimistic about the guild's future. In 1976, the percentage of professors who rode the tenure line nationally was 55.8 percent.[5] In 1989, it was 46.8 percent.[6] In 2007, it was 31.2 percent.[7] In 2021, it was 23 percent.[8] Notice a trend?

These data points mesh seamlessly with another set of gloomy figures. In the same period, there have been massive increases in the percentage of non-tenured professors—47 percent in 1987, to over two-thirds (68 percent) in 2021.[9] The non-tenured go by many titles and designations (e.g., part-time faculty, Contingent faculty, lecturers, adjuncts, postdocs, professors of the practice, etc.). In Chapters 2, 3, and 4, I will explain to you what all of these terms mean. Yet, the point is clear: the ranks of the non-tenured are swelling.

The problem isn't that there aren't any jobs for academicians. There are *plenty* of jobs, after all student enrollments are booming. The problem is that the jobs are *odious*. The majority of positions off the tenure track pay poorly—roughly minimum wage in many cases. They offer little or no job security. All of these factors summate, I repeat, to degrade the classroom product that we deliver to the "end user" (i.e., the undergraduate).

I anticipate that the death blows to tenure will arrive soon. The carnage will begin at public universities in Red States with Republican supermajorities. These legislatures will scale up their practice of "de-tenureification." It consists of clawing back a title that has *already* been conferred upon professors. Attempts to take tenure away from the tenured—once an extreme measure reserved for Russian spies, convicted pedophiles and the like—are ratcheting up in states like Indiana, Tennessee, Florida, Ohio, and Texas to name but a few.[10]

Surely, de-tenureification will receive a huge boost from the MAGA movement's gleeful penchant for firing public employees. As I write this book, tens of thousands of federal workers are being laid off by a unit known as the Department of Government Efficiency (DOGE). The DOGE ethos, I suspect, will soon migrate from the federal government to state houses. Intrepid cost cutters will go looking into the personnel files of scholars at public colleges and universities, in search of:

1) Tenured professors whose whereabouts are completely unknown
2) Tenured professors who do very little teaching
3) Tenured professors who teach very poorly according to the metrics college administrators use
4) Tenured professors who publish no discernible scholarly research
5) Tenured professors whose published research is mind-numbingly obscure, incomprehensible to all but specialists, or just sounds weird
6) Tenured professors whose scholarly research is stridently partisan (or not to the GOP's liking)
7) Tenured professors who share their anti-MAGA hot takes on X, Meta, Bluesky, their WhatsApp group chats, yardsigns, and so forth

These criteria, when taken together, cover roughly 102 percent of the faculty at any college or university in America. I teach at a private university, but if the criteria above were applied to me, I don't see how I could make it past number six. I've never felt that my research is stridently partisan. But as the DOGE experience teaches us, in America today there are no firm principles or objective standards; there's only the raw exercise of power.

A second tenure-destroying practice is more of a blunt force operation. States such as Texas and Indiana have recently proposed all-out bans on tenure at public universities—as in, *no one* gets tenure ever again.[11] These initiatives failed, but not by much. Given the persistence of the modern GOP, we should eventually expect them to succeed.[12]

If and when public universities abolish tenure, then this will leave only private universities as the defenders of this institution. Surely, the brave administrators at those schools will preserve the institution of tenure. Surely, those administrators will fight for a foundational scholarly right, one that enhances democracy. Let's turn to that now.

The Betrayal

Under Donald Trump's watch, the situation for professors is likely to worsen, and rapidly at that. I repeat, however, that the pain we've experienced and that we are about to experience is *not* mostly Trump's doing. In many ways, it is "our" doing—a combination of betrayals and bad decisions. I want to first talk about the betrayal.

"Administrative bloat" is a term used to describe an unusual development that has occurred in American higher education over the past three decades. It refers to the increasing devotion of university resources not to researchers and instructors, but to administrators. To give you a sense of the scale of this shift, consider the following: between 1976 and 2018, the number of administrators and other staff grew by 164 percent and 452 percent, respectively.[13] By 2017, it was noted that many schools were spending twice as much on administration as on instruction.[14]

Before going further, let's be clear as to what types of administrators are under discussion. I have no indictment to make of lower-level admins. Academic existence is impossible without them. There is just no way to run even the smallest department (and that department is, invariably, the Department of Comparative Literature) without someone skilled in scheduling and budgets, not to mention a host of professor-specific "people skills" that need not detain us here.

When I carp about administrators, I am talking about the proliferation of *upper* administrators: the exponentially multiplying deans and deanlets who replaced the professors as the undergraduates' major "point of contact" with the school; the ever-growing roster of provosts who selectively regulate the faculty; and the presidents and vice presidential staffs that have grown so big their suites occupy entire buildings. Let's not forget the legal back offices created to defend the university from all manner of litigation, while keeping a watchful eye on the professors (who, I confess, can get into some real trouble—and not always "good trouble").

It was these administrators who over decades made the decisions that would break the back of the academic labor force. Their most sinister accomplishment was this: finding ingenious ways to maximize the number of professors teaching undergraduates at the lowest possible wage. And the market, glutted with more and more underemployed PhDs every year, offered up countless opportunities to underpay scholars.

Which brings us to the betrayal. The upper admins were usually not corporate "suits" or outside consultants hired to "augment efficiencies" and "reduce redundancies." No, the majority of individuals who participated in the "casualization" of academic labor *were academicians themselves*. They went to graduate school for a decade and pounded out an unreadable dissertation, like we all did. They taught freshmen and sophomores, and sighed "*What's with kids these days?*" like we all did. Maybe they wrote a book or two. They were one of us.

They then accepted jobs in administration and proceeded to ratfuck their brethren.

In what other profession do the workers routinely ascend from the rank and file and then turn around and demolish their own vocation? When beat cops are promoted to detectives, do they immediately downsize the police force and look for ways to hire part-time labor? Does the newly appointed nurse manager proceed to recruit new hires in all hospital units to work for the lowest possible wages?

That's what our upper admins did to us. This was a fratricide, professors cannibalizing professors. It is not surprising that a national trust deficit has developed between professors and administrators; we don't trust these people.[15] They don't trust us either—and I concede that I sometimes understand why.

The Bad Decisions

As a guild, we scholars have made some really bad decisions. The one I linger on in this book was our decades-long devaluation of undergraduate instruction. We drifted into a position in which we treated college teaching as, at best, an afterthought. At worst, we convinced ourselves it was an impediment to our own intellectual development as scholars. This phenomenon is endemic at the elite schools, which I refer to as "Destination Colleges" (please note that my indictment of professors does not extend to those who labor, nobly, at community and junior colleges).

How we, as a guild, worked ourselves into a theory and practice of debasing college pedagogy is a complicated story. It's a story this book tries to tell through data analysis, comedic literary nonfiction, fictional vignettes, and the occasional human interest story. All these genres echo the same themes. We willfully abandoned undergraduate teaching. We let the admins decide our students' fate. And they did. In the worst possible way.

It was a dereliction of duty on our part, a guild-wide moral failure, one that had significant repercussions. Take, for example, the importance of advocacy. In order to advocate, we will need to make the case for our profession. We'll need to communicate with people who are not scholars. We'll need to articulate our desire not to be deported for making controversial statements within our area of expertise. We'll need to explain the dangers of paying professors less than minimum wage.

The problem is that few of us possess the ability to communicate beyond our specialized domains. Even though about one and a half million people in the United States are employed as professors, only a few thousand ever routinely connect with larger audiences on large print, media, and digital platforms.[16] So many scholars lack that ability and desire to connect with non-experts. You know how you develop that ability? By toiling day in, day out, with undergraduates. If you can connect with some hungover twenty-year old who doesn't know what a rotary phone is, you might be able to convince Joe SixPack to not defund the local U.

And then there is the loss of our organic "base." By stiff-arming undergraduates, we severed our natural connection with our constituents (i.e., the cohort of Gen X, Millennial, and Gen Z undergraduates who populate/d our classrooms). In turn, something fundamental has changed in professor/ student relations over the past half century. The encounter is now far more transactional, anonymous, and distant. While some undergraduates develop meaningful professional connections with a professor or two during their years on campus, most do not.

There doesn't exist a groundswell of admiration or respect among undergraduates for their teachers. True, students might march with professors to protest a given political issue (like anything involving Palestine; see below). But I don't foresee students marching with professors, en masse, to protect tenure or faculty wages. Once the DOGE's Red Cavalry rides onto state campuses, I sincerely doubt the students will "have our backs." Not because they hate us, but because their experiences with professors were so unmemorable.

Conceiving of ourselves as "experts," as opposed to "educators who are experts," that was the decision that helped bring us to our knees.

The Prism

The book you are about to read was written a decade ago, but its core arguments, I believe, are just as relevant today. Wherever possible, I updated and tweaked some chapters, but the central ideas remain the same. Colleges and universities, I argue, are complicated places, strange places. They reliably produce a good deal of dark hilarity. Much in the way that certain dull neighborhoods are "naturally occurring retirement communities," all campuses are naturally occurring campus novels (we'll discuss that comedic genre in Chapter 1).

To help outsiders make sense of what is really happening in college, this book suggests looking carefully at professors. Focus on the professors: how they are trained, how they labor, how they are (under)employed, how they think, how they suffer, and how they engage with students.

If you view higher ed through this professorial prism, I guarantee that you will think differently about how to select a school. You might also reassess your convictions about all the things we scream about when we talk about college today. I'm referring to those culture war issues that become the stuff of national headlines or congressional investigations (e.g., DEI, tenured radicals, allegations of censorship, etc.). Permit me to offer some examples of how adopting this lens might nuance your views on some of these flashpoints.

As I write these words, Columbia University appears to have surrendered ignominiously to a list of demands made by the Trump administration. Among them, the storied school was ordered to place its hard left, pro-Palestinian, anti-Zionist MESAAS department (i.e., Middle Eastern, South Asian, and African Studies) into "receivership" (receivership is sort of an academic death sentence whereby departments lose autonomy).[17]

This shakedown is likely unprecedented in American history. The federal government is demanding that a *private* educational institution monitor, and effectively sanction, the work of its own rigorously selected scholars. Columbia caved in because failure to do so would result in the revocation of $400 million of government grants.

Many Columbia professors are furious at their administration, and rightly so.[18] Columbia is a sublime seat of learning, in possession of substantial cultural and political cache. Surely, its $15 billion endowment could absorb $400 million of losses.[19] Legal observers believe Columbia would have prevailed in court, had they bothered to fight back.[20] Nevertheless, its leaders succumbed to wanton federal bullying. An administrative ratfuck indeed.

I mentioned earlier that everything is more complicated than it seems in higher ed, and the Columbia case is no exception. What the Trump regime is doing is abhorrent from the perspective of free speech (and other perspectives). But this shouldn't obscure how the professoriate's bad decisions factor into this controversy. The Columbia liberal arts faculty exemplifies the massive ideological imbalance that prevails at elite campuses across the country.

Like so many top-tier schools, Columbia's tenured and non-tenured ranks are pervaded by scholars beholden to a diverse array of far left academic theories and worldviews. In the humanities and social sciences these scholars vastly outnumber their remaining colleagues. This remainder includes a shrinking, graying cohort of liberals, a minute contingent of conservatives, and a few stray individuals whose thought defies political classification.

I don't mean to say that Columbia's innumerable leftist professors aren't solid scholars. I do mean to say that, ideologically speaking, the majority of them all inhabit a similar and predictable anti-Western, anti-American, and anti-Israeli space. The problem on Morningside Heights, then, isn't a problem of quality, it's a problem of *quantity* and *balance*. Certain ideological positions are vastly overrepresented while others are scarcely visible; this overrepresentation is evident at nearly every top school in the country.

How did such an imbalance occur (please note that this imbalance exists in the liberal arts, *not* business schools, STEM disciplines, most theological seminaries, and so forth)? The professorial prism I mentioned above offers all sorts of answers. The domination of the radical left at elite liberal arts faculties has a lot to do with administrators who aren't doing their jobs (Chapter 5). It has a lot to do with "search committees" that get commandeered by faculty members who wish to clone themselves (Chapter 7). It has a lot to do with scholars who have retreated to the cozy safety of their ideological snow globes

(Chapter 9). It has a lot to do with experts who gave up on communicating their ideas to laypeople (Chapter 1). It has a lot to do with professors who feel they can best advance their politics by working with *graduate* students (Chapter 9) and hence ignore undergraduates (every chapter in this book).

Conservative critics who contemplate this mess tend to get it all wrong and at the loudest decibels possible. They sometimes speak of a "liberal" bias in higher ed (note to conservatives: the radical left hates liberals *far* more than they hate you). When right-wing muckrakers do focus on the radical left, they focus on the *wrong* radicals.[21] An irony I can't get into here is that the far left intellectuals who really dominate elite faculties *have quite a few things in common with conservatives who love to lambaste elite faculties* (e.g., a suspicion of science, a hatred of liberal democracies, a mistrust of secular forms of governance, a dislike of individualism, an animus toward "rights-based" discourse, a fondness for politically charged mass religious movements, be it political Islam or the Christian Right; I could go on).[22]

My point? My point is you shouldn't believe the hype—from the right, from the left, from the college PR departments. Believe the professors, or at least this professor, assuming you find him trustworthy and not completely unhinged. When you look at higher education through the lens of the professoriate, you may gain a much more textured understanding of what is happening at our universities. Such knowledge might equip college shoppers with the tools to make better decisions about a monumental investment of time and money. It might also help explain why our profession is so doomed, why so few people want to be professors anymore.

INTRODUCTION
THE LANYARDS OF DESPAIR

I'm a **Full Professor** who teaches at a prestigious, almost flouncy, **R1 University**. Even though I was **tenured** a quarter century ago, no pretentious **Assistant Professor** can call me **"Dead Wood"** (yet). That's because I still churn out **peer-reviewed research** with a serene joylessness that rivals the affect of deli counter meat slicers.

I test run the **articles** and **chapters** in my **pipeline** when I deliver **working papers** at **academic conferences**. Oh, the conferences! These take place in stadium-sized exhibition centers located in cities I would otherwise never visit. During my allotted quarter hour of speaking time I relay to my audience (of seven people) the fruits of roughly 1,200 hours of research. This will be followed by a five-minute Q&A session in which someone's **Trailing Spouse** invariably delivers a six-minute manifesto. There's no Q, only A; his oration appears to be completely unrelated to the content of my remarks.

I daze-shamble out of my **panel** alongside a throng of **Contingent** and **Non-Contingent Faculty**. We are all looking for *meeting halls in which other incomprehensible, poorly attended* **talks** *are about to begin. Some of these rooms are named after the state flower or a deceased governor. To an outside observer, our frenzied movements in search of Iris 6 or Blanton 8 must resemble the murmuration of starlings. To an insider, however, these academic get-togethers could be likened to a massive killing field strewn with thousands of underemployed* **doctorates** *zombie-shuffling about the premises. These scholars have labored for ten, twenty, thirty years—and still have no gainful employment. Their lanyards lie askew upon their breasts. Their name badges, like mine, could just as well read: "How the fuck did it come to this?"*

***

How the fuck *did* it come to this? The beleaguered professors of my generation are pondering that. The ceaseless labor, the utter obscurity, the meddlesome, dipshit administrators, the right-wing demagogues claiming we provide material assistance to terrorists—this is not what we signed up for in **graduate school**. Back in the 1980s and 1990s, professing the Humanities evoked images of doing good, serving the commonweal, and advancing knowledge. We professors imagined we would soar like condors, not murmurate like starlings. Scholarship was about the plenitude of spirit. Scholarship was an endeavor both counter-cultural and noble. Scholarship made the world a better place. Or so we thought.

The generations of doctorates who have come after us see our concerns as frivolous, the academic equivalent of "First World Problems." For younger academics, it's not so much that the job isn't good. Rather, there simply are no good jobs. This is because colleges and universities will no longer sustain our plenitude of spirit, nor our way of life.

How things have changed since the 1970s. During that Golden Age, nearly 56 percent of American professors possessed **tenure** or were on the **tenure track**.[1] Being tenured virtually guaranteed a scholar lifetime employment and membership in the lower upper middle class (and since the mandatory retirement age for professors was done away with by Congress in 1994, the gig could last until you checked into hospice care).[2] Today, that Nixon-era number has been sliced by more than half (roughly 23 percent) and is rapidly trending downward.[3] Some pessimists predict that by 2040, the percentage of tenured scholars in all fields will sink to 10 percent.[4] Others believe the institution of tenure will cease to exist altogether.

What has happened in the intervening half century? One answer: greed. Colleges and universities have endeavored to drive down costs. Instead of making **freshly minted PhDs** eligible for tenure (which is expensive), American schools are increasingly employing them as expendable **adjuncts** (which is much, *much* less expensive). In another disturbing twist, colleges are hiring more **non-tenured full-time professors**.[5] What's the difference between all of these bolded terms? Read on, diligent GenX/Zer or millennial! All this stuff is on the quiz.

If you are among the 20 million or so Americans who are in college, or paying for college, or applying to college, now may be a good time to give ear to the theme I am propounding here.[6] For along with **graduate students** and **Post-Docs**, these adjuncts and non-tenured full-time professors who do most of the teaching are the shock troops of college pedagogy. It is they who are sent Banzai-charging into America's immense, restive, undergraduate population. It is mostly these scholars who staff the **gateway** and **service** courses, as well as the other **massified** classes the tenure-line folks don't wish to teach. This exploited, poorly compensated, labor force is responsible for the overwhelming majority of **undergraduate contact hours** in the United States. To review: poorly paid teachers/no job security/ teach a lot/go Banzai-charging. Tenured professors (disappearing) teach a lot less.

This absurd arrangement is especially pronounced at "Destination Colleges"—the one hundred or so elite, Blue Chip, Name-Brand schools in the country. They are distinct from the nation's other 3,500-plus institutions of higher education where students matriculate because of geographical proximity, or low cost, or specific vocational degrees they can procure. The Destination Colleges, by contrast, are the Dream Schools— applicants would trim their sails to the winds of hell in order to get into them.

But before applicants start futzing with the mast, spar, rigging, gaff and boom, I ask them to consider this: at these prestigious places the most accomplished and well-paid professors are kept far away from the undergraduates. Put differently, a Dream School's most valued scholars (i.e., those on the tenure line) are likely completely disengaged from the paying customers. The least valued scholars (i.e., the adjuncts and non-tenured full-time professors) usually do most of the teaching. Parents and their kids, gasping for breath under the crushing weight of loans and debt, must also be wondering how the fuck it came to this. How can institutions charging $65,000 a year in tuition treat teaching as an afterthought? Aren't they in the business of educating undergraduates?[7]

The mystery. The word-and-thought–defying mystery that is a college campus. The things that happen here are so difficult to understand. Nothing is quite as it seems.

We're going to see that it is very difficult to know how undergraduates are actually educated in American college classrooms. A provost can tell you exactly how many kids in the junior class are from South Dakota (a cohort whose presence on campus always inspires curiosity and awe), but she won't be able to tell you in any depth about what transpires in those **lectures** and **seminars** that they attend.

What little we do know about the classroom, however, suggests that students are being inadequately educated. A recent, influential study concludes that for most undergraduates "gains in critical thinking, complex reasoning and written communication are either exceedingly small or empirically nonexistent."[8] A university president rehearses, but does not dispute, the allegation that: "The mission of undergraduate instruction is increasingly subordinated to research and to work with graduate students."[9] An influential Harvard report diplomatically suggests "a collective 'reboot' of undergraduate teaching across the Arts and Humanities."[10] Reflecting on teaching standards across a wide range of institutions, two journalists sigh: "All in all, it's pretty poor."[11]

I ponder these misfortunes during stormy **departmental meetings** and the endless deliberations of the **Faculty Senate**. At these gatherings, by the way, there is an alarmingly high likelihood that we will spend ninety minutes debating where to house the Campus Compost Heap Initiative. I wonder about our fate while fulfilling my copious **Service** obligations, be they on the **admissions** or **grievance committees**.

I contemplate our plight when I participate in (increasingly rare) **job searches** for tenure-line professors. Each advertisement we place elicits hundreds upon hundreds of applications. Invariably, the committee becomes fixated on one candidate from a **Top 5 Graduate Program**. Look at this guy's **publication record**! Look at his Ivy bloodlines! His **doctoral adviser** was our **chairperson** Oswaldo's doctoral adviser! To lure him here, let's offer him a **reduced teaching load**. No, let's excuse him from teaching responsibilities altogether for his first three years! Let's call him now, put out a feeler, give him the old wink and nod. My **micro-aggressive** motion, that we Snapchat him the Official University Dick Pic, is seconded, then rejected by a vote of 7-2 (which reminds me that I ought issue a **Trigger Warning**).

In May, when I participate in yearly **commencement exercises**, my mood darkens even more. For it is there where my thoughts become as lined up and sorted out as the graduates marching in front of me. To the accompaniment of music, fanfare, and pageantry, I reexperience the Great (Un)Truth of American Higher Education. By this, I refer to the immense distance between the lofty rhetoric proclaimed by academic leaders and the base things they actually do. Word and deed, aspirations and actions, orotund pronouncements and actual achievements—these exist in a tensile relationship on every campus in the nation. With the possible exception of the corporate sector and organized religion, no institution can rival our own penchant for sanctimony, hypocrisy, and doublespeak.

Encased in their **academic regalia**, the dignitaries up front at the podium intone platitudes. They are droning on about "a posture of hope and empathy," "transforming the world through thought and action," or "forging minds in the classroom." But behind them, among the seated individuals colorfully robed, there are always a few incorrigible malcontents like me (also there is, without exception, a person who is knitting a sweater, but that is neither here nor there). We in the back row know the backstory. We perceive the distance between lofty word and base deed, like bus drivers cycling between the glittering tourist district and the shadier parts of town.

There is, however, one dimension of my professorial being that never induces outrage, regret, or despair. Let me begin, then, with a stunning confession for a tenured professor: I like teaching college students. More shocking still, I enjoy passing my days in the company of eighteen- to twenty-four-year-olds. Sure, they come to seminars in pajamas. Sure, they smell like gum. Sure, they trudge around campus double-fisting mammoth colorful Stanley Tumbler™ water bottles that would sustain them on a trek across the Nairobi Desert ("Gotta hydrate, professor!"). But I like them, nonetheless.

Now that they are practically running my classroom discussions—all because of **Active Learning techniques**—I enjoy working with them even more than I did when I started a quarter century ago. And I liked it a whole lot back then (when all I did was subject them to the **passive learning model** and yell at them for not appreciating the cinema of Éric Rohmer, or knowing who he was). My days, admittedly, are bereft of systematic or rigorous moral contemplation. Yet, the sincere effort to educate others well strikes me as a feat of conscience, a defiant political statement chalked in front of the Registrar's Office, a mitzvah.

I don't want to foster the impression that I am the sole soul on the Quad who loves teaching and laments its fading role in our institutions. My sense is that maybe ten to twenty-five percent of college professors in the liberal arts share my convictions. These educators are seated with me in that metaphorical back row. They recognize with bitterness the gap between what schools say about "forging minds in the classroom" and how little they do to make it actually transpire.

I profess solidarity with these Scholar-Teachers. It makes no difference to me whether they are tenured or non-tenured. I couldn't care less if they are bowtie-wearing Neo-Cons, or Far Left radicals sporting eyeglasses so aggressive they appear to be equipped with scythes. It's irrelevant whether they teach at Stanford or Where the Fuck Is That Place State? These are "my people." We, the educators, are the future of the Humanities. We are the only ones who might save the University (from itself). In all likelihood, we will fail. But, it's the posture of hope and empathy that counts, no?

Who knows, maybe those of my confession will change the hearts and minds of all those other scholars, the remaining seventy-five percent. At present, the Academy virtually forces them to spiritually and emotionally disconnect from teaching. We'll see that as tenure-track professors are "**climbing the ladder**," they must avoid undergraduates as much as possible. During one's **probationary period**, which usually lasts about six years, one endeavors to publish absurd quantities of research. As such, young professors develop an allergy and aversion to undergraduates. The mere existence of a sophomore—a needy timesuck who demands to be educated—is a looming menace to a probate's survival.

That poor sophomore is oblivious to the existential threat she poses to a professor's well-being. As with seniors, juniors, and freshmen, as with most Americans, she knows next to nothing about scholars. This is understandable. For starters, professors are generally neither interesting nor comprehensible. Further, the institution they work for is, by design, impossible to understand. To an outsider, everything about college, as the bolded words above indicate, is a daunting exercise in misdirection. My hope, throughout this book, is to demystify your professors, what they do, and the institutions they do it for.

There is no shame in being befuddled by Liberal Arts professors. But there is a risk. We may not be interesting, or comprehensible, but we are important—at least to those who take our classes. My surmise is this: your college experience, your college investment is rendered worthwhile or inadequate by your encounter with professors. As far as the success or failure of your education is concerned, our performance in the class is more important than the football team with the really shiny, Robo-Gladiator uniforms, the dorm rooms with skylights and heated floors, or the Belgian Ale Garden.

Presidents and governors can call us out. The board of trustees can slash instructional budgets to the bone. Administrators can subject us to **post-tenure review**. But they can't avoid the fact that a formidable or failed education depends on *us*. No, they can't take that away from us. Do you intend on making an informed decision about which college to attend? Do you wish to not fritter away hundreds of thousands of dollars in tuition? Do you want your, or your child's, college experience to not suck? Then you'll really need to learn a thing or two about us. And about us a thing or two you are going to learn.

**

This is a book about the woes of the American professoriate. These woes, I insist, directly affect undergraduate education. Put differently, our woes are *your* woes.

This is *not* a book about the failures and shortcomings of college students. I will not complain that they party too much, drink too much, sext too much (or too little). Nor will I nostalgically aver that my generation was better, brighter, more conscientious than this current crop of dipshits. Year after year, decade after decade, an American professor's duty is roughly the same: to educate a new batch of eighteen- to twenty-four-year-old dipshits. Each graduating class has its own pratfalling inanities. Each has its own vaulting ambition and somersaulting genius. I think TikTok is stupid, much in the way my professors in the 80s thought Sony Walkmans were stupid. But those opinions are completely irrelevant. It's not our task to judge the generations we teach, but to figure out how best they learn.

This is not a book solely devoted to elite institutions and elite professors. I won't draw generalizations about all scholars on the basis of my experience working at Georgetown University. I have spent more than half of my career laboring at less tawny addresses. I started professing at a public community college when I was twenty-four years old. From there, I brought my fierce adjunct energy to the BA-granting, broke-down palaces of the besieged, criminally underfunded, CUNY system (and what an instructive solvent of an elite worldview that was!). After seven years of a job that inspired me and materially impoverished me, I won the lottery in the form of a tenure-track position at Hofstra University on Long Island.

When my former paramour, Serendipity, led me to Washington DC in 2005, my cloak of invisibility was suddenly removed. Schools that had previously shown zero interest in my work now invited me to deliver lectures in my area of expertise. But why? I was exactly the same scholar that I always was?

As I trundled across the country, I started seriously thinking about professors and their passions. My talks were often delivered at institutions whose names I did not previously know. I know them now. I respect them now. The time I spent (drinking and gossiping) with their faculties has led me to a key insight: *professors of the Liberal Arts are remarkably similar to one another, no matter where they teach*. This simple reflection, which shall detain us at length, is deceptively significant. College shopper, consider this very carefully as you weigh the merits, sticker prices, and scholarship offers, of a school ranked 1 versus another ranked 150.

This is *not* a book about the collapse of colleges and universities. For the truth is that Higher Ed is doing just fine. STEM disciplines are thriving.[12] Business majors are booming.[13] The forecast for most institutions and their lucrative new curricular products is promising. Sure, a dozen or so schools capsize every year. But most others are sturdy vessels. It's the guild of Liberal Arts Professors *within* those institutions that is keeling like the Spanish Armada at Gravelines. What I want college shoppers to understand is that this tension majorly impacts them. Attending a great school with a miserable faculty is a terrible investment.

This is *not* a book meant to energize political partisans. What follows is not a Man of the Fringe Left Intervention, a 120,000-word disquisition intended to "map out the imbrications between the Neo-Liberal state and rising tuition through a Agambenian reading of *U.S. News & World Report*'s National

Universities Ranking." What follows is not a right-wing screed for the privatize-it-all crowd. Quality, affordable, public education—that is something we should make available to all of our citizens, is it not?

Let me, then, make another confession. As regards the political dimensions of my subject matter, I am uncertain, even a bit confused. I know for a fact that the professoriate is terminally ill. But I do not know precisely how to measure, and parcel out the blame. Did we commit suicide? Or, were we murdered? Or both? The answer, as we shall see, is not entirely easy to discern.

My objective is to explain to college students, prospective college students, and their parents why professors can and should be exceedingly relevant to their lives. I want to empower applicants to make informed decisions about where they will spend their post-secondary years. I also want professors *and* their detractors to confront some unpleasant questions. Like: does the institution of tenure actually serve the interests of students *and* scholars?

In the pages that follow, I will guide you through the strange and unseen habitat of the American Liberal Arts Professor. We'll begin by looking at how professors are built and trained in graduate school. Then, we'll examine how they are employed (or underemployed) by the institutions they serve. From there, we will figure out how all of this affects undergraduate education. I will assume the role of the "voiceover" in the nature show, the one dispassionately clarifying to viewers why the female alpine ibex is scampering up the side of a cliff with a dozen, snorting males in frenzied pursuit. Pity that poor ibex. Pity the professors. Pity the undergraduates.

In the process, I aim to rally "my people" around the noble cause of educating the Great American Undergraduate. I promise never to use the phrase "the life of the mind." There will be no guff about mounting "a Defense of the Humanities." I only will refer to "critical thinking skills" once. Clichés have served us poorly. College is a place where words suffocate deeds. Now it's time for candor, the unspeakable truth.

1

FUDDY DUDDIES

Every New York City cop, Tom Wolfe observed in *The Bonfire of the Vanities*, is Irish. Regardless of whether the police officer is Black, Latino, or Jewish, each one displays "Irish machismo… the dour madness that gripped them all."[1]

Wolfe's reflection inspires me to draw an analogy: every scholar in the Humanities is a Fuddy Duddy. We might be cinema studies experts in skinny jeans. We might be political theorists unfamiliar with the existence of collar stays. We might be art historians wearing statement scarves like a carapace. No matter—each and every one of us is a Fuddy Duddy. A brainy lunacy grips us all.

A Fuddy Duddy, to repurpose Zadie Smith's wicked burn in her novel *On Beauty*, is "someone who is a professor of one thing and then is just so *intensely stupid* about everything else."[2] This definition, I concede, may require greater nuance and elaboration. So, let me add that the Fuddy Duddy displays a staggering lack of Emotional Intelligence. Understanding/caring what anyone else is thinking or feeling—that's hard for us.

Even this clarification leaves us with many questions about the ways of the Fuddy Duddy. Fortunately, we have another source that sheds light on our subject matter. I refer to the "Campus Novel"—a category of Anglo-American fiction that has provided an encyclopedic compendium of Fuddy Duddy archetypes for nearly two centuries.

From its origins in Nathaniel Hawthorne's 1828 *Fanshawe*, to modern classics such as Francine Prose's 2000 *Blue Angel*, the Campus Novel genre has taken inventory of core scholarly traits. The Liberal Arts professors featured in these works are absent minded, aloof, delusional, incoherent, introverted, mercurial, paranoid, petulant, self-absorbed, self-important, self-obsessed, selfish, vindictive, and quite often, totally insane. To wit, Fuddy Duddies!

No faint shade on the spectrum of our dysfunction remains unilluminated by the campus novel genre. There is the *Clueless Fuddy Duddy*, like Doctor Mehlmoth of the aforementioned *Fanshawe*. He is a man so removed from this world that he fears loading a gun because "I know not accurately from which end proceeds the bullet."[3] There is the *Incompetent Fuddy Duddy*. Professor Welch in Kingsley Amis' *Lucky Jim* is described thusly: "How had he become Professor of History, even at a place like this? By published work? No. By extra good teaching? No in italics. Then how?"[4]

The *Megalomaniacal Fuddy Duddy* is a staple of the genre. Morris Zapp of David Lodge's *Changing Places: A Tale of Two Campuses*, is a cutting-edge literary theorist. He dreams of producing a scholarly tome about Jane Austen so comprehensive that it would succeed in "inexorably reducing the area of

English literature available for free comment, spreading dismay through the whole industry, rendering scores of his colleagues redundant: periodicals would fall silent, famous English departments be left deserted like ghost towns…"[5]

The darker dimensions of the professorial soul are explored in works like J.M. Coetzee's *Disgrace*. There, a scholar of Romantic Poetry sexually accosts a student in his class and triggers her psychological collapse.[6] Anne Beatty's 1989 *Professor Romeo* offers an even deeper dive into the psyche of the lecherous professor. Her cautionary tale takes place at the height of the "*an A for a lay*" era that peaked roughly between the 1960s and 1980s.[7]

The Fuddy Duddy appears prominently in literary narrative. Yet, she or he is invisible in the promotional narrative that American Higher Education spins about itself. Thus, when college PR departments rave about their "world-class faculty," they do not appear to have Fuddy Duddies in mind. Their counter-narrative envisions a professor whose studies enlarge the sum total of human knowledge. The fruits of her research are shared selflessly in the classroom. Emotionally available to all and sundry, she mentors every co-ed whose last name begins with the letters A-H. Coaches the field hockey team too. As evidenced by her million-dollar smile in glossy brochures, she photographs well.

But which fiction about professors is more accurate: the fiction of the flacks, or the fiction of the fictionalists? I vote for the latter. Novelists have homed in on a verity apparent to even the dopiest sophomore: *there is something objectively and uniquely bizarre about the academic persona.*

The perceptiveness of campus novelists is undeniable. Yet, they offer little insight as to *how* we all became Fuddy Duddies. My own lifelong study of the problem—and my long life being part of the problem—leads me to propose a theory. My theory points to graduate school as the source of our idiosyncrasies, the fount of our misery. To understand the woes of the professoriate (and those of undergraduates) look at how we are trained. Our training virtually guarantees that we will struggle in the classroom and that our students will suffer. One day soon, I plan on submitting the forthcoming findings to the double-blind peer-reviewed *Journal of Fuddy Duddy Studies*.

Graduate School Stage 1: The Master's

Graduate school is like Fuddy Duddy boot camp—if boot camp were to drag on for ten years, fifteen years, or indefinitely. It is here where apprentice scholars develop the attitudes, worldviews, habits, and mental ideation that will shape their professional demeanor for decades to come. It is also here where we learn to divest ourselves of empathy, sociability, and the ability to communicate with others. All of those virtues are expunged by the time we don our doctoral hoods.

Graduate school begins, promisingly enough, with the master's degree. Receiving that credential does not take inordinate amounts of Time and Money—those scowling divinities of occidental civilization. True, one may incur debt chasing this credential. Then again, every year tens of thousands of people get jobs partly because they've earned an MA in something or other. Signing up for a master's, then, is a risky-but-plausible economic investment.

As for time, the whole ordeal is demanding, but not in a preposterous or demoralizing way. Some master's degrees can be had in twelve months. Most take two or three years to complete. The entire process seems "doable." The goal seems scaled to actual human abilities. The end is always in sight.

All of which may account for why the vibe in master's-level courses is generally upbeat. The classes are full of shiny, young-ish people. These go-getters are training for bright futures, ascending into new economic quartiles and whatnot. Lots of secondary school teachers pursue the MA as well, useful people every last one of them. There may even be a handful of under-graduates registered for these courses—overachievers whose precocity and youth lend a hopeful spirit to the proceedings.

Most grad students view the master's as their own "terminal degree," the highest academic credential they ever intend on receiving. They decide that they have taken out enough loans. They decide that they would like to spend more time with their friends, family, and partners. To put it bluntly, they decide that "school" is over.

But not Fuddy Duddies! We decide to pursue the doc-torate—a decision that contravenes prudence, pragmatism, common sense, fiscal reality, leading economic indicators, fam-ily values, and the Social Contract. Even in the 1970s, when tenure-track positions could be had with ease, there was good reason to think twice about becoming a professor. Among those reasons, we could list the long hours, the stagnant salaries, the specter of living in some crappy college town, and, of course, other Fuddy Duddies.

By the mid-1990s, the academic job market began its pro-longed, and most likely irreversible, crash and burn. The decision to get a PhD makes less sense now than it ever did. Junior Fuddy Duddies, then, are like boat owners who ignore nautical warn-ings, flip off the harbor master, and sail into a squall. This being said, I reiterate that the MA phase is not where the infection sets in. We develop our defining characteristics not during the short summer of master's study, but after long, brutal doctoral winters. It is to those seasons grim that we turn to now.

Graduate School Stage 2: Coursework

If the completion of the master's took roughly three years, then the time needed to attain a PhD defies prognostication. The standard doctoral curriculum is divided into two periods of unequal duration. The first and shorter is called "coursework." The second and longer is often dubbed "writing." A combined five-year stay for both phases (added on, of course, to the earlier years pursuing the MA) is considered exceptionally brisk—a quickie! On average, an apprentice Humanist will labor for nearly a decade![8] Nearly half of all PhD candidates, I am dismayed to report, *never* complete their doctorate.[9]

Coursework usually lasts at least two or three years. The regimen a student follows is fairly similar across institutions. You attend a few seminars a week. These small classes are unlike the ones you took toward the MA. They are airless, and technically complex affairs. Few people sitting around those seminar tables are shiny or accelerating into bright futures. There won't be any fresh-faced undergraduates in these dense and demanding sessions.

My experiences during two tours of duty in doctoral programs were fairly commonplace. During coursework, I registered for three offerings per semester, totaling about eight hours a week. Excelling inside those classes was contingent upon consuming immense quantities of texts outside of those classes. As a general rule, every hour of class time necessitated three or four times that amount of preparatory reading. One ought not conclude, however, that a doctoral student spends a scant thirty hours a week behind a text.

A novice Fuddy Duddy intuits that this is not enough. She discerns that professional Humanists are bibliographical extremists. She recognizes our core conviction: only by ingesting insane quantities of text can a scholar *begin* to acquire true knowledge. She also takes note of our fetish for comprehensiveness. We are aroused by the fantasy—and it is a fantasy in every sense of the term—of being able to read *everything* about our subject matter. So, figure, forty to sixty hours a week are spent reading.

It follows from this that a doctoral student is a master of solitude. No one has of yet figured out how to make the act of reading a social endeavor. Aside from public rituals and prayers, it has been this way, I gather, since writing systems originated in the Bronze Age. The first phase of doctoral study, then, is where we become acquainted with our lifelong companions: isolation and loneliness.

One might demur that graduate students in the Humanities and Liberal Arts are expected to teach. Is graduate school not a plum opportunity to interact with other human beings in the form of undergraduates? In theory it is, but in doctoral practice, it is not. This has much to do with how American higher education undervalues classroom teaching. Professors, as we shall see, slough off instructional responsibilities whenever possible. Doctoral students are forced to fill that void. Naturally, they resent spending time away from their research projects.

Factor in that graduate students are neither intellectually, nor pedagogically prepared to teach undergraduates and you have the makings of a perfect storm: poorly paid, poorly motivated, poorly trained, and highly distracted twenty- and thirty-somethings conscripted to teach kids the same ages as their little brothers and sisters. The one possible opportunity for doctoral students to deal positively with people is effectively poisoned.

In any case, after a couple of years or so, "coursework" starts to wind down. You then pass a few modern language exams. These are usually in German, French, Italian, or other languages in which scholarship on your subject matter is published. You also need to take comprehensive written exams. When the comps are done, you are now known as "ABD," which is shorthand for "All But Dissertation."

Congratulations! You are ready to transition from coursework to writing. This is tantamount to being transferred from the general prison population to solitary confinement.

Graduate School Stage 3: The Writing Stage (The Fatal Inward Turn)

I've read accounts of rock stars who were so strung out on drugs that they claim not to recall a single thing that happened in their lives from, let's say, 1976 to 1979. All Fuddy Duddies can relate. We know what it's like to become disassociated from empirical reality. Each of us, after all, has researched and written a doctoral thesis.

The doctoral thesis, also known as the dissertation, is the crowning accomplishment of one's graduate career. It's like a book, but one that only three people will probably ever read. It's like a book, but one with more footnotes, indexes, and bibliography than actual text. It's like a book, but it's not really a book: To get it published, the author must substantially rewrite it and turn it into another book *after* the doctorate has been conferred upon you.

In order to complete the dissertation, you are honor bound to try and devour *every printed word* any other scholar ever wrote about your chosen topic. In theory, you must know as much about your subject matter as anyone else *and* say something about it that no one else has said before. You won't succeed, and you just might die trying. But along the way, you will become oblivious to the world around you. From 1988 to 1991, I was so entombed in monographs, articles, and ancient languages that those years are now a complete blank to me. Did Dukakis win?

During the writing phase, you learn how to think *small*. "Every rookie grad student wants to write a thesis about a subject as wide and grand and towering as a sequoia tree," complained an adviser of mine, an oddball Egyptologist. "The truth of the matter," he sniffed, "is that the final research product must be as narrow as a toothpick." He was correct. The writing stage of the doctorate is about slivering your interests down to a topic of ludicrous specificity.

The slivering induces a new type of solitude. During coursework, the isolation was spatial. During writing, it is both spatial and mental. You have no conversational partners. No one else is interested in your area of micro-specialization. Worse, no one else can fathom how it could possibly interest you.

Doctoral programs in the humanities are ivy-covered factories minus the smokestacks. They manufacture Fuddy Duddies—a formidable, but defective product. These women and men are built to engage with languages, documents, archives, and any permutation of "text" you can imagine. They evince a heroic commitment to their craft. In terms of "quality control," the factories perform superbly. They mint junior scholars who are genuine experts in their micro-specialized subjects. Charlatans and quacks, by contrast, rarely make it off the doctoral assembly line.

I have now drained my reservoir of nice things to say about this industry. For, as intimated above, doctoral training subjects young Humanists to a psychologically debilitating and intellectually scarring ordeal. It might not surprise the reader to learn that there is something approaching a mental health crisis in our graduate schools. A recent study at Berkeley University found that "47 percent of PhD students...score as depressed."[10] The number was 64 percent for candidates in the Arts and Humanities.[11]

Aside from the psychic damage they inflict, the doctoral mills poorly serve the most basic needs of undergraduates. A recent study lamented that PhD students "are learning in their graduate programs to deprioritize and perhaps even devalue teaching."[12] I will take this observation one step further. Doctoral study inculcates mental orientations that make it almost impossible for PhDs to *ever* succeed in the classroom.

During dissertation research, apprentices are forged into granite monuments of incommunicability. They are stripped of the skills necessary for engagement with *any* sort of audience. Graduate students are never trained in practical rhetoric or how to speak in public. They are never taught how to write. Most importantly, they are rarely taught how to *share* knowledge, to make it comprehensible for learners. One might say that the entire graduate experience teaches one how not to teach undergraduates.

Which is unfortunate because, as it so happens, *the primary function of most colleges and universities in the United States is to teach undergraduates.* There is then a bewildering disconnect between the supply of Basic Fuddy Duddies churned out by the factories and the demands of American higher education. An incongruity of that magnitude could only happen in fiction, in the make-believe world of a campus novel.[13]

Manfreds of Bavaria: A Campus Novel

While sifting through the 120-volume D. Martin Luthers Werke: kritische Gesamtausgabe, a twenty-eight year doctoral student in history thrice chances upon the name of one Manfred of Bavaria. Intrigued, the exhausted and slightly depressed ABD consults a few standard reference works. He then heads over to the copying machine to print out what little had been noted about this obscure figure in the dusty encyclopedias, dictionaries, and handbooks of the non-digital era. Ever since he completed his coursework, he feels he has developed an odd intimacy with the copying machine. He sort of likes the warmth of its engine, which he senses through his jeans as he bears in to line up the perfect copy.

Toward the end of his life, Martin Luther, the great Reformation theologian, maintained a short, spirited correspondence with an enigmatic polymath named Manfred. Their epistolary raged for roughly eighteen months, from 1543 to 1544. Then, inexplicably, their quills went silent. In his letters, Manfred's tone was weirdly binary. He could be dry, pedantic, and stiffly formal in some communications. But in others, his prose was frenetic, daft, and wildly inappropriate (e.g., he couldn't stop talking about Ulrich Zwingli's "small Swiss balls"). This dualism delighted and enraged the mercurial Luther who, as students of the sixteenth century can tell you, was a bit of a character himself.

The doctoral student mentions his findings to his favorite professor, over mugs of fair trade coffee. "Ah yes. Man-fred," intoned the sage as he massaged his own knee (he had suffered from joint ailments for years). He draws out the syllables of Manfred's name as if paying homage to a great artist known strictly to initiates. "Strange fellow that one. Was he an Anabaptist? A crypto-Catholic? I've always been curious about that dude. He sure got Luther's goat, I'll tell you that much. Actually…I don't think anyone's published. Hey! You know what? You should write your thesis about Manfred."

Oh heart a fluttering! Oh ten philharmonics blasting a Mahler scherzo all at once! Oh eternal spring day! The grad student was elated. And not only because his sixty-eight-year-old mentor employed the word "dude" in his presence. After the coursework stage, students spend years scouring the earth at their feet for suitably microscopic dissertation topics. Some never find their theme and tumble from the doctoral orbit like flaming space junk. Others settle on subjects so broad, unwieldy and complex that they virtually consign themselves to mental illness and heart disease. But this lucky son 'a bitch just had his toothpick handed to him—and by the past president of the Middle States Society for the Study of the Reformation no less!

As the ABD prepares to embark on the odyssey that is the writing stage, he is consumed by a vision: one day, all Reformation scholars shall refer to him, with reverence, as The Manfred of Bavaria Guy. He's going to own Manfred.

That will be his vindication. That will be his I-told-you-so to mankind broadcast as a sort of Amber Alert on everyone's mobile phone across three time zones. When he started pursuing the master's at age twenty-two, his friends—of which he had many—were supportive, but skeptical. By the time the twenty-five-year-old was accepted to a leading doctoral program (one of eight in the country widely considered to be in the Top 5), they practically staged an intervention to keep him from enlisting and starting coursework. In spite of grave warnings about the state of the "academic job market" (a clown from his weekend kickball team always made spasmodic air quote gestures when pronouncing that term), he accepted the offer along with its $10,000-a-year stipend. To him, that seemed like a lot of money.

Ready to launch into the writing stage, the twenty-eight-year-old charts an accelerated course that will lead to his triumphant thesis defense in just three years' time. And what strange victuals he will bring along for the ride! He is packing huge cardboard boxes and burlap sacks of emotional emptiness. Friends, family, movies, his hipster kickball crew—unless it pertains to Manfred, it is not coming aboard.

Only his girlfriend, a shy web developer, is on the manifest. Three years back, she completed her MA in Film Studies and realized, astutely, that school was over. It happened when she accidentally wandered into an "Evangelicals in Tech" convention, held adjacent to a dreary gathering of the Modern Language Association at some massive exhibition hall in Nashville. During a casual conversation with an infectiously upbeat young engineer named Audrey, she had a secular epiphany of sorts. As Audrey was telling her something or other about coming to Christ, she spontaneously decided to take up coding.

Six months of study and $30,000 tuition dollars later, she was properly credentialed. Scarcely a week would pass without a recruiter seeking her out on LinkedIn. Ah, the bliss of possessing a marketable skill! Paying off her student loans quickly, she moved effortlessly from one well-remunerated job to another. No threat to her boyfriend's solitude, this serene young woman can spend hours on end reading texts on screens or watching French art-house cinema. She's his ideal stowaway.

His launch into the writing stage, however, is a bit delayed. Comprehensive. He must be comprehensive. Just doing prep work on his thesis requires twelve months, not the six he had originally allotted. Half a year is spent culling every written word about Manfred. Another six months is spent mastering sources about the German-speaking milieu of 1530 to 1550. He never imagined there would be so much relevant scholarly literature about that.

Just shy of age thirty, he heads to the archive. He's "going in." According to his Doktorvater (i.e., lead thesis adviser), this is the experience that separates the professional researcher from the mere reader. The septuagenarian scholar describes this labor with unpublished documents in obscure languages as the "purist manifestation of scholarship there is." Any journalist, or cleric, or dentist can have their opinions on Luther. These imbeciles sometimes do. But genuine, scholarly, knowledge is only acquired through this type of painstaking intimacy with original sources.

It's true! When the ABD is in the Manfred archive in Aschaffenburg, which smells faintly of B.O., he feels pure. He imagines himself as a monk, or like those ancient Egyptian priests who plucked every hair off of every conceivable surface of their flesh. The long hours in this moldy sepulcher have demanded sacrifices—of his social life, his eyesight, his physical well-being. But in return, he is learning things about his subject that absolutely no one else in the field has ever known.

One thing he learns is that there once existed another scholar who studied exactly this—another Manfred of Bavaria Guy. An elderly librarian casually mentions it to him while handing him a dusty folio. But phew! That researcher, fortuitously, stroked out in 1992 before he completed his doctorate.

*While scouring parish registries on his thirty-second birthday,
our ABD makes another discovery, and this one will change his life.
Not only did there exist another Manfred of Bavaria guy, but there
existed another Manfred of Bavaria! There were two Manfreds!
Old man Luther (and posterity) seems not to have noticed that he
was corresponding with two different individuals, only one of them
was obsessed with Zwingli's junk. Luther, on the lam from popes,
selling out Anabaptists, and bickering with seditious peasants, was
too distracted to draw the distinction.*

*The finding elicits euphoria. The apprentice feels as if he has
deciphered Linear B, or refuted a longstanding claim of Shake-
spearian authorship. He's going to be the Manfreds of Bavaria
Guy! He skypes from Aschaffenburg to share the good news with his
fiancé. She, in turn, has her own good news to share: she's pregnant.*

*Soon enough, however, that first blessing becomes a curse. Every
assumption he made about "Manfred" in the past four years needs
to be verified afresh. Which Manfred was which? The introduction
must be rewritten. His chronologies are way off. The five existing
chapters he wrote all need to be revised. Upon return to the states,
he postpones his thesis defense until the following spring.*

*And then: catastrophe. He is asked to teach an undergraduate
class. His Doktorvater has just won a Guggenheim. The program's
ace grad student, naturally, will be the understudy. An outsider
observing the moment his professor broke the news at the coffee
shop, might be excused for concluding that one man was sharing his
diagnosis of stage four esophageal cancer with his son.*

*The preparation for HIST 090, "Early Modern Europe," is
tedious and always done in haste. The forty assembled students
(seventy-five are registered) seem impervious to the charms of the
1540s. They yawn during his lectures. As he rambles on in a mono-
tone, they are obviously messaging one another on their laptops. He*

faintly registers the smiles and chuckles rippling across the lecture hall like whiplashing dominos, especially when he draws any event occurring in the Reformation or Counter-Reformation back to the Manfreds—something he does with great frequency.

One day, a precocious sophomore—some sort of religious scold he always thought—asks him, rather pointedly, about the St. Bartholomew's massacre.

"The St. Bartholomew's massacre? Of 1562? Lucy [her actual name was Evelyn] you're mentioning that because—"

"1572. It happened in 1572," Evelyn corrects him.

He suddenly realizes he knows little about this landmark event other than a whole lot of Huguenots were murdered and somebody famous was thrown out a window in Paris. He's coasting entirely on his recollection of the movie "La Reine Margot" starring the luminescent Isabelle Adjani.

In academic culture, there is no greater shame than not knowing something in your stated area of expertise. Nothing short of godly omniscience is demanded of the specialist. This is why professors are hesitant to mount a direct challenge to the factual accuracy of another professor's claim. To do so is tantamount to declaring war, or making a martyrdom video. When such conflicts do occur, the vanquished have been known to lapse into depression, resign their posts, apply for high school teaching jobs. But a student correcting a professor—very rare, but it happens—is the greatest form of scholarly degradation conceivable.

1562 or 1572? The room falls silent. Whoever among the students spells "Bartholomew" correctly will Google the right answer first. The episode is attaining the theatricality of a standoff. In a panic, he goes the Full Fuddy Duddy and dismisses the entire event as "a minor episode solely of interest to FUCK-ing Fundamentalists." When he pronounces "FUCK-ing," it's as if a hidden sound engineer amplified the words with extra gain, bass, distortion, and reverb.

Well, no one's smiling or chuckling now. The students are aghast. They look like they have just witnessed the St. Bartholomew's Day massacre in full. Even the attendees with the neck tattoos, the pink hair, and the ear gauges—the ones who roll their eyes whenever the religious woman chimes in with her subtly anti-Catholic strictures—are crestfallen. He'll feel their wrath, he knows, on his course evaluations and ratemyprofessor.com. But the truth is that he just doesn't care. He's a scholar, not a teacher. Teaching is messy, dirty. Only research is pure.

His final trip to the archive, at age thirty-four, yields modest returns. The second Manfred, the pervy one, remains a perfect riddle. Who was that guy? Our fellow is out of energy. Dead in the water. His partner is complaining about having to support the young family on just one salary. In despair, he petitions to schedule his doctoral defense. His advisers, mindful of his age (advancing) and resources (limited), accept. Like all doctoral candidates he doesn't feel ready. He feels like a fraud. He hasn't even entered the "fake it" stage of "fake it 'til you make it." There is so much more research to be done.

At the defense, his family by his side, his three examiners begin by praising him for his "seminal discovery." But then, in accordance with ancient Humanistic traditions, they descend into a trance-like rage. Even the mildest mannered Fuddy Duddy transmogrifies into a mace-swinging Berserker during the doctoral defense. They heartlessly pick his dissertation apart. His mentor leads the charge and could just as well be outfitted with nun-chuks. A grad student in anthropology once told him that the doctoral defense is a rite of passage. Humiliation precedes initiation.

After two hours on the rack, the candidate, his girlfriend, and his sleeping two-year-old daughter (not named Manfredia—she drew the line) are asked to leave the room so that his advisers can confer. Seated on a fraying couch in the hallway, the dissertation writer stares into space. He's stunned that one of his examiners asked him about the St. Bartholomew's Day massacre of 1572.

His fiancé, for her part, is having another epiphany. She saw her partner "reframed" as it were. In this context, he looked different. Watching him meekly absorb those blows in that room full of pretentious scholars leads her to new insights. He has changed. It's as if he has erased an entire side of his personality, taken this fatal inward turn. Why does he never make eye contact anymore? Why has he shaved his head in the shape of tonsure? Why is he so docile, so solicitous of his advisers?

Oh my God, the advisers! She's seen unpleasantness in the workplace. But nothing could match the pettiness and vitriol of that dissertation committee. Especially that idiot with the cane—what did that endless story about his "defrocking" as president of the Middle States Society for the Study of the Reformation have to do with anything?

When she freelanced at a start-up, the frat boy banter of a few coworkers made her uncomfortable. At another company, she once witnessed a coked-up VC crack a laptop over a snarky coder's head. In each instance, she simply quit and found another job. There were plenty of options. But where do scholars go when they can stand no more? What opportunities do they have? She tears up when she suddenly realizes that the father of her child, twelve years into his studies, has no other options.

After twenty interminable minutes, his examiners reemerge from the chamber as their old selves. They hug the thirty-four-year-old man awkwardly—for there is no more peculiar hug than those academicians bestow upon one another's soft misshapen bodies. There will, they caution, be a few required revisions. But by next semester, he should be done and ready to apply for positions in his field. Between the MA, coursework, and the writing stage, he will have spent only twelve years in grad school—a quickie! Regrettably, there was only one nationally advertised tenure-track job in Early Modern Europe this past year.

His girlfriend gives him a desultory kiss and heads back to work. He fails to notice how curt and freighted her "goodbye" sounds. His child awakens with a shriek just as he contemplates the changes demanded by his advisers. He'll get it done by September. Then, he estimates, he'll need about two more years to revise the dissertation into a publishable work of scholarship.

2

WHO IS YOUR PROFESSOR 1? "THE NON-CONTINGENT"

"Professor Grimsby's the Department Chair, right?" a clueless junior asks me. She's desperately searching for the chairperson, the only person authorized to sign off on her petition for study-abroad credits. Professor Grimsby, I proceed to inform her, is a splendid classroom teacher. He has published some really thoughtful research. Good guy, too!

He is not, however, the Department Chair. I don't tell her that Dr. Grimsby is what is known these days as "Contingent" faculty. In terms of institutional power-and-prestige dynamics, he's the opposite of the Chair. He serves at the pleasure of our Chair, Dr. Lowry-Turns, a mopey Associate Professor who sits barricaded in her office all day.

What I also don't share with the junior is that even by Fuddy Duddy standards, Grimsby is one Grade A Oddball. He refers to himself in the third person as "the Falconer." He cuts his own hair in the men's room and offers passersby a "free trim." He's a recumbent bicyclist. He recumbent-bikes to work. Memorably, he once recumbent-biked down the third floor hallway, parting a sea of astonished and appreciative Comp Lit majors.

He parks his various rigs outside his office door, right by the staircase. The contraptions are always gleaming with moisture, as if they possessed sweat glands of their own. This, apparently, perturbs Dr. Haynes, a Full Professor. We became aware of Dr. Haynes's displeasure, indirectly, when our department was issued a $10,000 fine. The storage of large objects proximate to a stairwell entrance is a Violation of Code, said the Fire Marshall. The hefty summons did not evade the notice of our Dean, who threatened to deduct the $10,000 from next semester's instructional budget. Which he subsequently did. Chairperson Lowry-Turns did not take that well.

As for our clueless junior who thought Grimsby was a Chair, she was just making a rational surmise. Grimsby the Contingent looks distinguished. For a man turning sixty, he's remarkably fit. As one might expect from the type of person who makes the lifestyle choices that Grimsby has, he's a trippy, unpredictable, engaging lecturer. Student laughter barrels outward from his classroom in muffled thunderclaps. He receives raves on official Student Teaching Evaluations and ratemyprofessor.com. The junior might also have noticed from his syllabus that Grimsby has published a fair amount of scholarly research.

Actually, he has published *more* scholarly research than some tenured Full Professors, like Professor Haynes (whose yearly salary is five times higher). I later learn that Dr. Grimsby once drew Dr. Haynes's attention to this fact. They had words. When enraged, every scholar is adept at using his or her words. Shortly thereafter, I found out that Dr. Haynes's brother-in-law is a Fire Marshall. Sigh. To spend your life in Academe is to witness an endless cycle of revenge killings.

But I am divagating. What's fascinating here is our junior's misperception about Grimsby. Like most Americans, she can't make any sense of scholarly hierarchies. This is because these hierarchies don't make much sense. Then again, undergraduates don't really lose sleep over this stuff. Most complete their degrees without ever knowing, caring, or thinking about the professional standing of any of their teachers.

My position is that students, prospective students, and those footing their college bills, really *should* know who's who on a college faculty. They should know this because issues of rank, professional status, and academic distinction are central to how American undergraduates are educated. Let me phrase this in even starker terms: unless you understand what types of professors a college or university is placing in front of students, you can't understand very much about that college or university.

The Two Tribes

One useful way for outsiders to make sense of the professoriate is to divide it into two broad tribes of uneven size. The smaller, better paid, and slightly less discontented cohort is known as "tenure-line," or "Non-Contingent" faculty. It consists of "tenure-track" and "tenured" professors. The much larger, poorer, and more discontented remainder is referred to as "Contingent" faculty. These non-tenurable Grimsbys go by many names and are often called, rather imprecisely, "part-timers," "adjuncts," "lecturers," and so forth.[1]

Though sometimes antagonistic, members of the Tribes can also be colleagues, friends, engage in sexual congress, and even get married. In truth, Contingent and Non-Contingent professors share common experiences. All went through the iron furnace of grad school and emerged as crisped out Fuddy Duddies. All are slaves to text. All are victims of self-imposed isolation. All evince huge deficits of Emotional Intelligence. It's a strange bond, but a bond, nonetheless.

Too, the professional boundaries between them are occasionally porous. Sometimes, a Contingent, usually on the younger side, gets a crack at tenure and ascends to Non-Contingent status. Sometimes, a tenure-track professor is denied tenure and joins the ranks of the Contingent. Though in most cases, such a scholar departs from Academe altogether.

Let's start by gaining a better understanding of those considered the lucky ones, the Hayneses who are on what is known as the "tenure line."

The Tenure Line

Tenure, or the realm of non-contingency, is a relatively recent invention. The system, as we know it today, was established when two groups, the American Association of University Professors and the Association of American Colleges issued the *1940 Statement of Principles on Academic Freedom and Tenure.*[2] Given that the first college in this country, Harvard, was established between the years 1636 and 1642, it took our guild three centuries to concoct this most unusual and spectacular idea.[3]

The idea went something like this. In order to flourish and contribute to the common good, a scholar would need "freedom of teaching and research and extramural activities."[4] This same scholar would also require "a sufficient degree of economic security."[5] To ensure expressive liberty and fiscal stability, the architects of the tenure system codified vague, but strict, guidelines to be followed by colleges and universities.

The *1940 Statement* expanded upon decades of previous proposals and initiatives. It also drew valuable lessons from conflicts in which opinionated, in-your-face professors learned how little job security they actually possessed. Before there was the tenure system, there were lots of scholars expressing unpopular ideas and getting chucked out on their keesters for their iconoclasm. Whether it was Jane Stanford (co-founder of the school) forcing a politically outspoken liberal professor to resign in 1900, or the faculty purges that occurred during World War I, and the McCarthy Era, the take-home lesson is abundantly clear: trustees, politicians, assorted powerful people, and just about anyone with a beef (and some sway) won't hesitate to destroy a professor's career.[6]

The 1940 document sought to tilt the balance of power to the professors.[7] It stipulated that a scholar hired by an institution would undergo a probationary period not to exceed seven years.[8] Before the seventh year, the school would make a final, love-'em-or-leave-'em decision on the probate's fate. The tenure system laid down fairly clear rules of the road, a road that forked off in two existential destinations for the professor: virtually irrevocable lifetime employment (i.e., tenure) or swift termination.[9]

If the school loved a scholar and thus granted him/her tenure, he/she would be "locked in," as it were. Such a person could no longer be arbitrarily dismissed or fired. According to the *1940 Statement*, any attempt to terminate a tenured professor would first have to pass muster with a "faculty committee and the governing board of the institution."[10] These scholars were now well protected from the Jane Stanfords of the world.

There is one curious thing about the 1940 Statement. *The text says nothing about what it takes to achieve tenure* during that probationary period. It's a silence so complete, profound, and crystalline, that contemporary readers rarely recognize its import. Over the past eighty years, the general national trend for achieving tenure has inclined in the direction of producing more and more (and more) peer-reviewed scholarly research. We'll get back to this in a moment, but for now the reader should appreciate that the original statement had no opinion on *how* tenure was achieved. It simply posited tenure as something that was beneficial for scholars, schools, and students.

The *1940 Statement*, with its "pithy propositions of lofty sweep" was "the prompter of a great *reform*."[11] In fits and starts, the tenure concept gradually gained currency among North American institutions of Higher Education. By 1973, "100 percent of established public and private universities practiced some form of tenure."[12] For the past half century, the quest for tenure has absorbed the passions, energies, brilliance, cunning, ego, and id of nearly every scholar in the Liberal Arts. With few exceptions, one pursues a doctorate with the express goal of joining the ranks of Non-Contingent faculty, of getting on the tenure track.

To get on the tenure track only to be eventually denied tenure is thought to be the most traumatic professional experience a scholar will ever undergo. But I can think of something more traumatic. Nowadays, the majority of scholars *don't even get a chance to ride the tenure track*. They are consigned to Contingent status forever; from the moment they receive their doctorate to the day they call it quits. That is why our way of life is collapsing. Scholars are trained across a decade in grad school (see Chapter 1) to compete for a scarce and finite number of jobs. But we are getting ahead of ourselves.

Assistant Professors

Tenure-line (or Non-Contingent) professors come in three flavors: crazed (i.e., Assistant Professors on the tenure track), crushed (i.e., Associate Professors who are tenured), and coasting (i.e., Full Professors who are tenured). Let's start with the blessed Assistant Professors.

Their blessing has to do with the miracle of being *hired* to a job that holds out the possibility of tenure. The statistical likelihood of this occurring is disturbingly low. My estimate is that in the Humanities, between 60 percent and 80 percent of doctorates will never experience this great good fortune. There simply aren't enough positions. Being hired to the tenure track, by the way, is different from being *granted* tenure—an epic slog that I shall discuss a few paragraphs yon.

What we should recall is that from the ABD period in grad school forward, every junior scholar hankers for that rare tenure-track position. If offered, a young PhD nowadays will usually take such a job *anywhere* in America. Even if—and this often comes to pass—the post is at some janky place ranked 300 to 400 slots lower than the Top 5 graduate program in which the doctorate was earned.[13]

Once hired to the tenure track, a scholar is usually referred to as an "Assistant Professor" or "junior faculty." She is then said to be "climbing the ladder" toward tenure. A standard contract is issued, and the novice is now "on the clock." As per the *1940 Statement*, this period traditionally lasts six years (though it can be shortened for a few years or lengthened in negotiation with a dean or a provost).

After this probationary interval is completed, the candidate will be subjected to "tenure review." A positive outcome of this lengthy and rigorous evaluation will land her a job for life—*for life*! Should her tenure committee, however, find her unfit she'll be asked to clear out her office within one year's time and never return. We live and die by the dictates of the *1940 Statement*.

I ask the reader to contemplate the stakes involved from the point of view of an Assistant Professor. If she gets tenure, she'll never have to apply for another job until she retires or passes away. Given that a scholar usually receives tenure between the ages of thirty-five and forty-five, this ordeal could extend for half a century! Would you sacrifice six years of your life to assure something like thirty to fifty years of stable and secure employment?

An Assistant Professor sure as hell would! She's already devoted ten years in graduate school to achieving this goal. By acing her six-year probation period, she will vindicate the sacrifices of that dreary decade. She's just won the lottery and chanced upon a tenure-track position. There is no turning back. There is no easing up. All systems are go. An Assistant Professor is "all in" (to herself).

The Formula

When hired, an Assistant Professor immediately gathers intel about something called "The Formula." It contains the true, albeit unstated, criteria employed by a school for granting tenure. We noted earlier that the *1940 Statement* did not elaborate on how tenure was achieved. Every school has its own standards, but at nearly every Destination College and many non-elite schools the lead criterion is clear: publishing insane amounts of peer-reviewed scholarly research.

The Formula is almost never put in writing. Even if it is, one should pay it no mind. That's because a written Formula at a Destination College would affirm that teaching plays a "substantial" role in whether one receives tenure. Unless the school's administration understands "substantial" to be a synonym for "largely irrelevant," or "worth dick" then this affirmation is false.

The Formula is usually divided into three broad categories: Research, Teaching, and Service (which refers to sitting on labor-intensive committees, participating in numerous one-off events, extra work with the community, etc.). When you are evaluated for tenure at a Destination College, *at least* 70 percent of the decision hinges on your publication record. This assessment of the quality of your research is taken quite seriously. It is not unusual for the entire evaluation to take eighteen months and include input from dozens of people as it passes through multiple committees, before landing on the Provost and President's desk.

Around year six, an Assistant Professor will submit her tenure dossier. It will contain an updated CV and copies of all of her publications. Ideally, she should have a few pounds of material to deliver. Quality is always swell, but in my experience *nothing beats quantity*. The committee that reviews your application is usually composed of people employed by your school. These arbiters are in your discipline but probably not in your super specialized subdiscipline. They thus can't make exacting decisions about the quality of your publications—that's left for the external reviewers.

These are scholars at other universities who study more or less exactly what you study. These might be people who love your work, or people you have loved. Or maybe they don't love you as much as they should. This accounts for why Assistant Professors are perennially friendly, even though they have no time for friendship. They are nice to everyone in their field who occupies a higher rank. After all, if your evaluators don't think much of your work (or you), your tenure case is probably doomed. Back on campus, probates will be scrupulously polite, deferential, and respectful with senior faculty who will be chiming in on their tenure decision. A sculptor commissioned to cast a statue reflecting the "Assistant Professor experience" would surely place the subject on his knees, head lowered, in the position of a winged supplicant, accelerating diagonally toward the flaming sun.

After Research, the remaining 30 percent of your tenure decision will be divided between Teaching and Service. Calibrated in this manner, Teaching can never trump Research. Never. Not once have I seen evidence of outstanding classroom performance redeem a candidate with middling research output and tepid external reviews. Though sometimes, justifiably, a scholar with an average research profile will be sunk by an odious teaching record.

With the Formula heavily weighted toward peer-reviewed publication, scholars adjust their behavior accordingly. During her period on the clock, the Assistant Professor has an interest in doing the following: 1) confirming her hunch that The Formula is insanely weighted toward Research; 2) revising her doctoral dissertation and getting it published by an academic press; 3) starting a new book project and getting that in print or, at least under contract by Year Six; 4) publishing as many peer-reviewed articles in as many leading journals as possible; 5) publishing a few chapters in scholarly books dedicated to a particular subject; 6) presenting papers every year at international, national, and regional conferences; 7) extending the hand of friendship to all colleagues on campus; and 8) ditto for colleagues off-campus since any of them might become external reviewers.

The Student and the Assistant Professor

Finally, we are ready to ask the really important questions: What about students? Where do they fit into all of this? The obvious and sad answer is that *they don't fit into any of this*. At an elite school, undergraduates have no useful or beneficial role to play in an Assistant Professor's tenure drama. If anything, students are a hindrance to promotion. As an aggregate, these little bastards need to be taught. This entails preparing classes (arduous), teaching classes (exhausting), grading papers (arduous, exhausting, and boring), and so forth. In short, students make demands on the time that an Assistant Professor has rationed for more essential tasks.

It is for this reason that probates do everything in their power to teach as little as possible. They scheme assiduously to get "release time" from classroom instruction. This planning begins even *before* they are hired. An example is provided by Andrew Hacker and Claudia Dreifus in their book *Higher Education?: How Colleges Are Wasting Our Money And Failing Our Kids—And What We Can Do About It*. The authors recount a disturbing, and all-too-familiar, tale.[14] A hotshot job candidate for a tenure-track position in political science at Queens College spends the better part of his interview preening, underperforming, and generally getting on the hiring committee's nerves. Undaunted, the applicant complains that his potential teaching load would be too large. Lacking Emotional Intelligence, he then proceeds to inquire about his sabbatical (which he laments should be granted every three years, not every seven years). Naturally, he neglects to pose any queries about "the school or its students."[15]

The authors are, understandably, outraged by the callousness of "Golden Boy" as they dubbed him. Yet, this behavior, when you see it from his perspective, is quite rational. In graduate school, you receive the tacit message that only losers teach a lot. The tenure Formula at most schools rewards research, not pedagogy. It thus makes perfect sense that you'll spare no discourtesy in trying to avoid the classroom.[16]

Actually, I have encountered much worse than Golden Boy (who, to Queens College's great credit, was ultimately not offered a job). It is not unusual to find young scholars who, upon being offered a tenure-track position, coolly inform their employers that they won't be reporting for duty just yet. Classes begin, let's say, in August of 2026. Yet, they request—or more accurately, demand—to defer until August 2027. This might be because they have external funding to complete a project, or have been offered some other plum, teaching-free, research opportunity. These scholars are such an awesome addition to the faculty that they can't even be bothered to join the faculty! This is the academic equivalent of being too sexy for one's shirt.

In my experience, the request to defer employment in order to conduct research is often a bluff—as noted above, there are so few jobs to be had. The candidate has been advised (by their doctoral adviser usually) to "push back." Or perhaps he has another job offer and wishes to play one school off against the other. The point of the exercise is to gauge how (un)serious a school is about teaching responsibilities.

And the answer to that question is "pretty unserious." Were a scholar to make such a request of a committee chaired by me, I would urge my colleagues to rescind the job offer. I'd call the candidate myself and tell him to go fuck himself, but in the nicest, most collegial way. In the upside-down world of Academe, however, the opposite often occurs. Hiring committees become even *more* enamored of their coquette. They revel in the prestige that comes from snagging "rising stars" from elite grad schools. The dean thus authorizes a year of leave for the new hire (before he has even arrived!). Professor Gap-Year won't set foot on campus until 2027. Would you be surprised, reader, if I mentioned that Professor G eventually asks for another extension into 2028?

Once an Assistant Professor has actually started teaching, it's more of the same. Elite colleges will often offer her "nurturing leave" for a semester or two.[17] Why would a college or university do that? Because its reputation centers on its faculty's publication excellence, not teaching excellence. And because... actually, I do not know why else schools do this. It defies logical explanation.

In the best of all worlds, the Assistant wins a fellowship or grant. This arrangement works on so many levels. The Assistant gets to shuck off instructional responsibilities for a semester or two. The Dean is on board because the Assistant's salary is now paid by the outside organization sponsoring the fellowship. Let's assume the supplicant makes $80,000 a year to teach six classes. With her salary paid for by some anodyne foundation, the Department can use the $80,000 to hire twelve adjuncts (at $5,000 per class, let's say) and trouser the remainder. Everybody wins! Except for the undervalued, exploited adjuncts. Except for students. Except for any Assistant Professor who actually likes to teach. For how does a year away from the classroom improve her teaching skills?

If an Assistant can't secure a fellowship or get release time, she'll soldier through. Customarily, she might ask for a reduced load. If her contract stipulates she teaches a "3-3" (three classes in the fall, three in the spring), she'll request to have it chiseled down to a 3-2. None of this, by the way, means that the Assistant Professor neglects her classroom duties. It's a buyer's market for college employers; they fully expect some modicum of pedagogical proficiency *from individuals who were never trained in pedagogy and have little time or incentive to cultivate that skill.*

Our Assistant Professor will teach a full slate of courses (i.e., usually between 4 and 7 per academic year depending on the school) while coughing out her endless flume of peer-reviewed research. Students will rate her performance on university-administered surveys. Senior colleagues will visit her class at least once a year and submit written evaluations (see Chapter 4).

The Assistant is acutely aware that her fate hinges on exemplary research, *not* exemplary classroom instruction. Inspired teaching and mentoring will *not* land her tenure. Conversely, a record of poor teaching may compromise her tenure chances, especially if her publication record is merely average.

This means that the Assistant Professor's orientation toward her classes is transactional, almost defensive. She will be prepared. She will rarely come late. She will grade conscientiously. On the downside, her conscientious grading might veer into inflationary grading. The last thing she needs is a junior stomping into her Chair's Office to complain about her. She will never under any circumstances say anything controversial while lecturing. She'll deactivate her sense of humor, assuming she has one.

Given that she has no time for her own friends and family, she will have even less time to meet students outside of her mandated ninety minutes of weekly office hours. Holding office hours is one thing—but mentoring is another. And there'll be none of that until after tenure review (maybe). Note to students: an Assistant Professor is not a good person to engage in a chat about what a jerk your boyfriend has been lately. Nor does she want to hear about the series you just binge watched on Netflix.

The professor's quest for tenure does, theoretically, have some advantages for students. If your professor is teaching a class in her area of specialization, she'll be a master of the subject. She's up every night until 3:00 a.m., writing and reading about this stuff. Few people on earth know it better than her. That's really beneficial for some undergraduates, especially ambitious juniors and seniors taking advanced seminars.

Then again, let's not oversell scholarly expertise obtained in the wee, small hours of the morning. The truth is that the Assistant's nocturnal investigations are far better suited to helping her educate *graduate* students. This is one of the many bewildering structural asymmetries of American Higher Education. Scholars are micro-specialists addressing micro-specialized questions. Undergraduates, however, have no compelling reason to be interested in those questions—or those answers.

Assistants are often assigned large entry-level classes with titles like "Introduction to American Literature." A micro-specialist researching Eudora Welty's late writings until the crack of dawn doesn't have time to bone up on John Cheever, or John Updike, or Toni Morrison. Which is too bad because they're on the syllabus too! And yet, seventy-five students sit at the knee of the sleep-deprived Assistant Professor who has forgotten that John Cheever isn't Raymond Carver.

Associate Professors

The rank of Associate, at most schools, designates an individual who survived the probationary period as an Assistant Professor and was granted tenure. The tenure system, as we shall see, pulps it losers. Upon the victors, however, it lavishes the perk of secure, stable employment until the age of retirement. Is there any other guild that so shields its members from the vagaries and vicissitudes of market chaos? Other than federal judges, what other class of American worker can bank previous accomplishments *forward* for decades on end?

All of this might lead one to imagine that the Associate Professor's defining characteristics are satisfaction and serenity. This is not the case. Associates are notoriously discontented. A recent survey of the three tenure-line ranks found that Associates were the least satisfied across *every single one* of the twenty-five criteria measured.[18]

Associates speak of "depression of postpartum magnitude."[19] They complain of being "overwhelmed and alone."[20] They feel that they are "workhorses" who are being "dumped on."[21] The nurturing period is over. The university now expects the newly tenured to sit on all sorts of committees, steward initiatives, mentor the next batch of would-be stars, and spend countless hours in meetings. Ought I mention that this time-intensive Service work is never compensated?

One anonymous complainant describes the transition from Assistant to Associate thusly:

> *When I was a newbie, I idealized the small town near my university, but it now seems a provincial, toxic wasteland. My office building used to seem shabby chic; now it feels dilapidated and smelly. I had tried to think of my colleague's ringing laughter in the hallway as cheery; now she just sounds like a hyena. Some colleagues I had tried to consider original or eccentric now seem just plain nuts. The brisk now seem brash; the quirky have become creepy.*[22]

Accounting for why Associates are "some of the unhappiest people in academe" is not easy.[23] Maybe it's because this person is entering the frame of life in which the self-indulgence (characteristic of the Assistant Professor) must *and can* take a back seat to the thankless performance of one's duties. Childcare, mortgage payments, ailing parents, testy partners, and other banal realities of Early Onset Middle Age hit the Associate Professor hard.

Or, could it be that the Associate Professor has simply *changed?* She entered grad school at twenty-five, and now she's forty-five years old. She no longer affirms that sacrificing three years of evenings, weekends, and summers to research a 9,000-word, peer-reviewed article is livin' the dream. She gets night sweats thinking about spending ten pre-semester days in August double-checking her footnotes. Suddenly, she hates what she loved and loves what she hated. I wonder if that's possible—that a person could *change?*

It's awfully hard, though, to change when you are manacled and fenced in. One of the rarely discussed drawbacks of our vocation is the utter lack of mobility that it permits. Associate Professors are more or less glued to their institutions. Sure, they can win some grant and spend an invigorating semester in Florence, Tokyo, or Marrakesh every few years. But should they opt for a change of scenery, should they grow tired of their campus and colleagues, their options are limited. Moving to another institution and keeping one's rank—what is known as a "lateral appointment"—is exceedingly rare.

I'd estimate upwards of 95 percent of tenured faculty will retire at the school where their talents were recognized. Deans in the Liberal Arts are notorious for taunting disgruntled Senior Faculty in the Humanities with the locution: "You're free to go elsewhere." These sons a' bitches know full well that there is no "elsewhere." There simply aren't enough positions.

In any case, the post-tenure period is when previously latent impulses come to the fore. Associates are notorious for undergoing Career Reassignment surgery. Some take law classes at night. Some start blogging about the seminal Hair Metal Bands of their youth. Others let their politics hang out—after all, they can't lose tenure for expressing their thoughts on pressing issues of the day. Research productivity often wanes, though these people are *constantly* working. Often, they are laboring on some vast bottomless project requiring the strength and focus of a person twenty years younger.

The phrase "terminal Associate Professor," with its cancerous resonances, describes that listless scholar whose career simply stalls. Elsewhere, these folks are called "tenure's mistakes."[24] I'd love to be able to say that many restless Associates finally settle down and discover their One True Passion: teaching. But I cannot say that because it is untrue. For nearly two decades, the Associate has been socialized into a culture where students are an afterthought. Why would she be compelled to change now?

Going to Full

If there is anything that motivates an Associate Professor, it's the desire to be promoted to Full Professor, the highest rung on the ladder. The sojourn takes anywhere from three to thirty years from the day one is granted tenure. Some institutions will crown a Full simply on the basis of her being a good citizen (or just not being an asshole). Others imbue the position with a donnish solemnity, the likes of which we'd expect from Oxford or Heidelberg in the nineteenth century. As such, *nothing* published before tenure was granted will be considered for promotion. These Associates who wish to "go to Full" have to start from scratch and reinvent an entire research agenda.

Those who do get promoted to Full have a psychological profile all their own. They are often referred to as "bullet proof." This is an allusion to the fact that they cannot be fired and can piss people off with relative impunity. The bullet metaphor reminds me that Fulls bear resemblances to veteran members of street gangs. Scarred and disfigured, Fulls have seen some shit, learned some lessons.

They have watched the tenure beast devour close friends, the chalk outlines of their cadavers emblazoned on the pavement in front of the new B-school building. They were standing right there back in '98 when the entire under-enrolled Assyriology department was wiped out by Dean Payne. Let's just say that Full Professors harbor no illusions about the nobility of the academic vocation. Fulls tend to be some of the most wizened, wily, and ambivalent figures on campus.

Some Fulls "buy in"—they wear the institutional lapel pin to work. They'll assume more administrative tasks and conduct less research. Their brain velocity will naturally decelerate, year after year, until retirement. Other Fulls display what can only be described as a unique academic superpower: the ability to disappear and never be around, ever. These scholars and others who contribute nothing are referred to as "Deadwood."

All things equal, a Full Professor isn't going to be spending much time with freshmen and sophomores. A Full's seniority entitles them to select the courses he wants to offer. Those are usually small, advanced undergraduate seminars or graduate classes. If they do teach "Beginning French," or "Basics of Linguistics," then it is likely due to a punishment or an epic horse trade. It's unlikely that a Full would teach such a course of his own volition. For his entire adult life, this scholar has been conditioned to view undergraduate teaching as an inconvenience. Why would he change now? And even if he did, what skills would he bring to the classroom?

***

Now that our survey of the tenure-line ranks is complete, it may be prudent to address one major misconception. In the popular imagination, professors are often held to be wine-and-cheese-eating, faculty-lounge-kibbitzing, good-for-nothing, layabouts. I hope the descriptions provided above belie these allegations.

In the future, professors are well advised to keep working hard; nationally, we are starting to see initiatives that claw back tenure privileges. Schools like the University of Tennessee are toying with a policy of "de-tenure."[25] Similar policies have been quietly creeping forward for decades, usually under the designation of "post-tenure review." The always-in-the-news University of Wisconsin has instituted a review of tenured faculty members that occurs every five years.[26] What appears different about the Tennessee and Wisconsin model is that the oversight for de-tenuring is being moved away from the Faculty Senate and toward administrators—a move that seems to contravene the *1940 Statement*.

Assistants, Associates, and Fulls are trained to conduct research and publish their findings. The scholarship they produce demands commitments of time that most normal folks would find unfathomable. This is no 9-5 gig, as any scholar's spouse or partner will testify. Nor is their salary commensurate with their monumental efforts. The time it takes to research and write a book chapter can vary from 200 to 1,200 hours. No matter how long it takes to craft that piece (and so many others), *a professor's salary stays the same*. The privilege of guaranteed lifetime employment obscures the fact that scholars ceaselessly perform unremunerated work.

So, let's not say that tenure-line Professors don't work hard. My contention is that *most do not and cannot work hard on their teaching*. That task is left for the other part of the tribe, the non–tenure-line, or Contingent, faculty who are mostly responsible for educating undergraduates. Let's meet them now and try to figure out if exposure to these scholars is good or bad for college students.

3

WHO IS YOUR PROFESSOR 2? THE CONTINGENT

Katelyn dreamed of attending Precious New England Liberal Arts Boutique College. She fell in love with the school upon reading a quirky, bestseller written by one of its surprisingly large detachment of tattooed anthropologists.

Her parents demurred. They urged Katey to consider the flagship campus of Big Bland State U. The affordable tuition was, admittedly, a factor that attracted them. But mom and dad were really hooked when they heard an NPR story about its psychology department's innovations in the treatment of eating disorders.

Katelyn's best friend in high school, Dylan, applied to Genteel Southern School With A Peculiar Antebellum Vibe. He did so after he chanced upon an acerbic *New York Times* Op-Ed penned by a curmudgeonly political scientist in its employ—a fellow who seems to have been born in a seersucker suit with a glass of Kentucky Bourbon in his hand. Dylan's parents accepted his decision, albeit with some dismay; they had hoped he'd attend Exquisite West Coast Top 5 with its slew of Noble Prize–winning economists.

In the nonfictional world, the fictional characters above based their decisions on what is known as "Strength of Faculty." This is a popular selection criterion for the college bound. It's perfectly understandable to fantasize about sitting at the knees of brilliant scholars. But permit me to offer Katelyn, Dylan, their folks, and you, my reader, a helpful tip: *Don't be surprised if the brilliant scholars and their surgically repaired knees aren't on the same continent as your campus when classes are in session.* (I can't dwell on it here, but professors, for some reason, have a proclivity for joint and bone complications.)

In most cases, the high-profile professors who burnish a school's reputation are nowhere to be found on the Quad. And if they are, they won't be kicking back with dopey freshmen like Katelyn and Dylan. The sleeved anthropologist will be doing fieldwork in Rangoon. The psychologists will be granted "release time" to draft a proposal for a three-year, multimillion-dollar research grant. The bourbon-swilling political scientist will be leading one graduate seminar per semester for God and Country. And the famous economists…I actually don't know what famous economists do…. Something with data sets, I would surmise.

It is for this reason that it is hazardous to select an undergraduate institution on the basis of its rock-star professors. It makes more sense to do this when you apply to *graduate* school. Though on this level, too, famous scholars tend to be nowhere in sight. Ah, delinquency: the recompense for recognized scholarly accomplishment!

I think it's better to think in terms of "*Adjusted* Strength of Faculty." What needs to be "adjusted" are naïve, outdated assumptions about who staffs undergraduate lectures and seminars. When using my ASF metric, please bear three operating assumptions in mind. First, consumers should recall that an institution's most renowned scholars rarely work with undergraduates. Second, students will spend *some* time studying with the school's (non–rock-star) tenure-line professors. Thus, they'll have a few courses with the Assistants, Associates, and Fulls whose lives and passions we just chronicled. The third adjustment is the most significant: undergraduates will probably spend a lot, if not the majority, of their class time with those who are neither tenured, nor eligible to be tenured.

Let's familiarize ourselves with these scholars, known as Contingent faculty. They comprise the larger, more poorly paid, and unhappier of the two professorial tribes. We need to figure out who the Contingent are and under what professional conditions they labor. As we probe the nexus between these Fuddy Duddies and the American Undergraduate, it will be of interest to examine how the Contingent stack up, *as teachers*, against their tenured counterparts. The plight of the Contingent, as we shall see, reveals much about the professorate's future. It also calls attention to the hypocrisy, even cruelty, of our institutions of higher education.

The No Longer Hidden Professoriate

"Contingent faculty" is a dehumanizing, imprecise, catchall phrase used to describe non–tenure-line professors. To wit, those who are neither on the tenure track, nor tenured. This term is rapidly replacing older, even less precise, nomenclature.

Back in the day, we used to speak of "adjuncts" or "part-timers." One study from the 1970s dubbed those we now call Contingent, the "hidden professoriate."[1]

Nearly half a century later, they're no longer hidden. The category has ballooned to immense proportions in recent decades. Something like 71 percent of professors nationally can be parsed under the Contingent designation. (In 1975, the number was around 44 percent.[2]) This means that *more than one million people* in this country labor off of the tenure track.[3] They perform most of the undergraduate instruction in the United States. They do all of the teaching at junior colleges and For-Profit colleges (where no one gets tenure). At Destination Colleges, they handle the majority of classroom duties as well. But how much?

Reliable, clear information about how much of an undergraduate's education is spent with Contingent faculty is hard to procure.[4] Colleges and universities tend not to be forthcoming with such data. It's not difficult to figure out why. Parents paying astronomical tuition, naively assume that their kids are studying with a school's most distinguished faculty (i.e., tenure-line faculty who often appear on talk shows). It's the job of two administrators, the Vice President for Strategic Communications working in tandem with the Director of Institutional Research to never unsettle that assumption.

There are a few studies that help demystify the work of Contingent faculty, like the report compiled by Center for the Study of Academic Labor at Colorado State University.[5] The CSAL offers general data on what percentage of a given school's faculty is non–tenure-line. These numbers provide, at best, indirect insight into what I think is the most important question raised by the Adjusted Strength of Faculty metric: *Of the forty or so classes a student takes in order to graduate, what percentage will likely be taught by Contingent faculty?* Still, studies like the CSAL report provide a baseline for those who want to get beyond meaningless statistics offered by college PR departments.

At the super-elite schools, the numbers vary greatly. At Harvard, 37.3 percent of the faculty are Contingent. At Yale, it's 53.3 percent, and Columbia is 61.5 percent. Then again, Princeton is at 29.9 percent, and Stanford at 32 percent.[6] At my school, Georgetown, the number is 68.3 percent.[7]

When we move from Research Universities to Liberal Arts Colleges, the percentages improve. The Top 5 Liberal Arts Colleges, according to *U.S. News & World Report* (e.g. Williams College, Amherst College, Swarthmore College, Bowdoin College, and Middlebury College) fall between 30.4 percent and 35.9 percent. We should also mention Pomona College with its impressive 6.3 percent of faculty being Contingent.[8]

Later, we'll talk about Historically Black Colleges and Universities and Women's colleges—they will be instrumental to our examination of alternative tenure Formulae. For now, please note the following: Spelman College is at 47.6 percent, Howard University at 52.3 percent, and Hampton University at 60.4 percent. For women's colleges, the numbers vary widely. Wellesley is at 39.0 percent, Smith College at 28.5 percent, and Scripps College at 10.2 percent. Meanwhile, Bryn Mawr is at 46.0 percent and Barnard College is at 58.8 percent.[9]

The figures above don't reveal how much time Katelyn and Dylan would spend in Contingent versus Non-Contingent classrooms en route to their degrees. They only tell us about the physical presence of non–tenure-line scholars on a given campus. These people usually teach multiple classes, which are very large and disproportionately on the undergraduate level. So, in the absence of better data, I'll offer an estimate, and an admittedly very imprecise one. My surmise is that at most Destination Colleges, between 40 percent and 75 percent of an undergraduate's instruction is delivered by Contingent professors. At cash-strapped public universities, the percentage is probably higher.

Is all that time spent with non–tenure-line professors a bad thing? Well, it's certainly an underreported thing. In order to determine if it is harmful to undergraduate education, let's learn more about the Contingent.

The Contingent of Hope

The term "Contingent" refers to all sorts of disparate scholars, at different stages in their careers, laboring under varied conditions. Tenured faculty, we saw in Chapter Two, come in three flavors: Assistant, Associate, and Full. When two deans at the University of Michigan undertook a study of their Contingent staff, they were surprised to find no less than *twenty* ranks on their campus.[10] The high number is probably because schools like to conceal their Contingent crisis; they often make up titles to sound more respectable like "Professor of the Practice of..." For purposes of analysis, I am going to divide up the Contingent into two categories: those who hope (somewhat plausibly) that one day they may get a crack at a tenure-track job, and those who have abjured all faith.

As for the hopeful, let's start with "graduate students." Typically, they are dragooned into educating undergraduates either as part of their scholarships, or in return for a small stipend. These candidates for the doctorate generally loathe teaching;

it severely disrupts their research momentum. Too, teaching is looked upon as drudge work—real scholars don't waste their time with college kids. Undergraduates are not unaware of this. They resent being taught by emotionally blunted introverts who obviously don't give a shit about them.

Similarly hopeful about their tenure prospects are "Post-Docs." When I started out in the 1990s this position was pretty rare, especially in the Humanities. Market forces, however, have conspired to make getting a Post-Doc a very common pursuit for those who have just emerged from the graduate school assembly line. Post-Docs (and Visiting Assistant Professors) are usually factory-fresh PhDs who applied for a bunch of tenure-track jobs but had no luck. They then enter another fiercely competitive contest. This time, the prize is a one or two-year stint at a Destination College. And this time they prevail.

The newly hired Post-Doc has earned the right to shelter in place at a reputable institution for a year or two. While there, 25 percent of his energy will be devoted to teaching, and 75 percent to research. An additional 25 percent will be spent applying for the handful of tenure-track jobs that open up every year. Another 15 percent will go toward looking for *other* Post-Doc opportunities, or visiting assistant professorships. It is not unusual for a rookie scholar to mount two or three valiant Post-Doc stands across a six-year span. Eventually, this itinerant Knight of the Curriculum Vitae will either slay contingency and win the tenure-track lottery or throw in the towel. From there, he can go into academic administration or descend from the Ivory Tower, slamming/raising the drawbridge on the way out.

The Contingent of the Damned

Which leads me to the far larger, less hopeful, slice of the Contingent pie chart. Those I have in mind have all effectively *given up on ever gaining tenured status*. They might go by different titles: "Instructors," "Lecturers," "Fellows," "Adjunct Professors," "Assistant Professors of the Practice of Teaching," and so forth. Like all Contingent workers, these scholars are attractive to universities in the following respect: they can be hired (and fired) for a song and they possess much-needed skills, like the ability to teach Freshman Composition, or Beginning Chinese, or Introduction to Psychology, or Statistical Methods I.

In the Fuddy Duddy mindset, as the reader may have gleaned, these are not the plum teaching gigs. As we noted in our previous chapter, rank determines how courses are assigned. Traditionally, the Full gets the choicest offerings (i.e., small seminars, courses on the advanced level) and few of them would ever volunteer for the aforementioned courses. Associates and Assistants get a mix of classes, some of which they like to teach and others that drive them to despair.

The Contingent get whatever is left. Whatever is left is usually referred to as a "Service," "Gen-Ed," "Gateway," or "Core" course. Whatever is left is overenrolled and filled with scads of freshman and sophomores—students who often need greater attention.

In and of itself, what I have just described is unfortunate, but not scandalous. So what if an adjunct teaches three sections of French Level 2, while a Full spends his semester facilitating the much more invigorating "Flaubert and Balzac"? A college has standards, right? If its rigorous vetting process has adjudged the Full to be worthy of tenure, then surely there must be some benefit commensurate with the Full's stature. Right? (Please see the next chapter for responses to these questions.)

This brings us to the scandalous part. Contingent faculty labor under conditions that range from bad to deplorable. A 2014 study found that the median pay per class (three credits) for a Contingent was $2,700.[11] Assuming one has the where-withal to teach ten courses a year—a staggering amount of work—one would be near the poverty line for a family of three or four, which, in fact, is roughly where the majority of Contingent Faculty appear to be situated.[12] It is estimated that 25 percent of part-time college faculty are on some sort of public assistance.[13]

Contingent faculty members lead harried lives. In order to make ends meet, they will string together a schedule of classes at a variety of area schools. These piecemeal laborers are often referred to as "gypsies," "nomads," "vampires" (because they teach lots of evening courses), and "freeway flyers." Such a scholar might teach "Microeconomics" at a top-twenty place in the morning. Then, she—nearly two-thirds of Contingent faculty are women; fewer men are enlisting in Academe—will drive across town and offer a modified version of that course at a community college.[14] After that, she'll work the night shift at some other seat of learning.

Aside from the low pay, being a Contingent faculty member rarely entitles one to long-term job security, retirement benefits, or health care. Accompanying the increase in Contingent scholars has been a heightened awareness of their mistreatment and misfortune. Over the past few years, media stories with titles like "*Professors on Food Stamps*," or testimonials such as "*How eBay Subsidized My Academic Career*," have appeared with gloomy frequency.[15] In 2013, a truly macabre story made the rounds about a Duquesne University adjunct professor, Margaret Mary Vojtko, who died in abject poverty, incapable of paying the bills for her home heating.[16] In 2016, Hamilton Nolan of the now defunct *Gawker* curated a series of posts in which Contingent faculty talked about their travails. As one contributor put it:

> *One of the things that is rarely discussed in regards to this issue, is that the quality of higher education has definitely suffered. Though many adjuncts are very good teachers, you can only offer so much when you are over-worked and underpaid. The frustration I felt toward the university made its way into the classroom. When I was grading papers, I had to remind myself to give less effort to each student—there simply wasn't enough time in the day to give them the attention they needed.[17]*

This observation is singularly relevant to the present discussion. Throughout this book I have been claiming that professors and undergraduates are inextricably bound. Thus, when colleges and universities treat scholars this way, it has *direct consequences for how well undergraduates learn.* Hiring Contingent faculty is a budgetary decision, no doubt. Let us never forget that it is a budgetary decision with tremendous pedagogical ramifications.

The Future?

Of late, a different category of professor has come to the attention of Higher Ed observers. This designation represents a sliver of the Contingent pie graph. But for reasons that shall become clear in a moment, this sliver may have massive implications for the scholarly future.

The workers in question are referred to as "Full-Time Contingent Faculty." They are not tenurable, but they are not part-time either (which is why calling Contingent workers "part-timers" can be inaccurate). Since 1975, part-time faculty went from about 24 percent of all total instructional staff to roughly 42 percent in 2011.[18] This other category of Full-Time, non–tenure-track has gone from 10 percent in 1975 to about 16 percent in 2011.[19]

The increase in Full-Timers without tenure that I am highlighting is modest, but its significance is potentially immense (some might say "catastrophic" and others "transformative").[20] This growing category presents one alluring, cost-efficient solution to a long term fiscal "challenge." The challenge is the tenure system, that costly, inviolable, staple of academic existence.

Please recall that when a university grants someone tenure, they are making a virtually irrevocable, decades-long, multimillion-dollar, commitment. You do the math. A scholar is tenured at age thirty-eight. Commands a salary of $100,000, plus generous benefits. Shuffles about the campus for, like, thirty-nine years. Retires at age seventy-seven, posing for farewell pictures in her walker with the bright yellow tennis ball feet. Factor in inflation, cost-of-living increases, etc. You don't need a calculator to recognize that a tenured professor represents a monumental financial investment.

Enter the Full-Time non–tenure-track worker. She is paid, let's say, $60,000 a year. Whereas other Contingent faculty members are hired on a semester-by-semester basis, the Full-Timer receives a renewable contract, ideally for stints of three-to-five

51

years.[21] She gets modest health benefits and maybe something toward her retirement. She does a good job. Is renewed.

Prior to the AAUP's *1940 Statement* (discussed in the previous chapter), this arrangement was referred to as "presumptive tenure." It was presumed that you'd be rehired every few years by a benign administration. And you were! Until one day you said something controversial and weren't. Which was awkward for all parties involved.

Some of us have the queasy sensation that presumptive tenure is the blast from the past that will emerge as our future shock. Surely someone with an MBA has done the math. One can just hear a trustee wondering aloud: "*Why bother tenuring people anymore? We'll just hire more Full-Timers without tenure. We'll save money. We'll be more nimble and responsive to changing student interests and market demands. Problem solved! And I don't care about the Faculty Senate and its stupid resolutions about "preserving the professional mechanisms that have sustained our success." "Neo-Liberalism" this, "Neo-Liberalism" that. You know what? I don't give a fuck about Neo-Liberalism, whatever it is.*"

Among scholars, the subject of the Full-Time Contingent elicits bitter, internecine strife. Purists, and devotees of the *1940 Statement*, fear that this type of employment augurs a new normal—a tenureless universe where "academic freedom" is nowhere guaranteed. The aggrieved will take the floor of the Faculty Senate delivering stemwinders about why this sort of hiring must be stopped.

Suffering adjuncts who make $25,000 a year and receive no benefits analyze the situation somewhat differently. Not surprisingly, they have no moral reservations about the specter of gainful, full-time employment. They politely request that the purists, particularly the *tenured* purists, screw their heads out of their asses and stop opposing the creation of more such positions.

Members of the administration, naturally, are right there with suffering adjuncts! For the folks over at Corporate who wish to further divide, conquer, and downsize our guild, this is one doozy of a wedge issue.

The Contingent in the Classroom

Adjusted Strength of Faculty is a buzzkill of a statistic. It implies that you'll never, ever, get to hang out with that evolutionary biologist who gave the really cool Ted Talk. It revivifies a childhood insecurity that super smart and talented people would never willingly hang out with the likes of you.

Adjusted Strength of Faculty also forces us to "get real" about who is educating our undergraduates. The reality is that the sacred act of teaching is increasingly performed by, and relegated to, overworked, long-suffering, and poorly remunerated Contingent Faculty. We are witnessing the dawn of a two-tiered division of labor at Destination Colleges and elsewhere: the most valued faculty conduct research, the least valued teach undergraduates.

What remains to be figured out is how all of this affects students. It is often assumed that tenure-line faculty do a better job of teaching than their non-tenured colleagues. In light of what we know, however, I think that proposition is arguable. So I ask without prejudice: in whose classroom will an undergraduate learn more? Under the tutelage of a Dead-Wood Full like Haynes? A Full-Time Contingent instructor like Grimsby? Or a melancholic Associate, like Lowry-Turns?

Ask the tenure-line people these questions, and they'll probably fall back on groundless institutional prejudices. They'll insist that "our guys" (i.e., the tenured and tenure-track) are superior in the classroom. After all, "we" hired these people. "We" entrusted them to work with us for, potentially, decades. And "we," indubitably, are the type of people who make Solomonic decisions.

Personal observation leaves me skeptical. I want to explore the possibility that Contingent instructors outperform their tenure-line counterparts. Unlike Assistants, Associates, and Fulls, they are unambiguously (though meagerly) incentivized to perform to the peak of their instructional abilities. To be a Contingent Faculty Member is to be acutely aware of how replaceable you are. These laborers are hired more or less seasonally. They are evaluated and rehired almost solely on the basis of peer and student evaluations. If they wish to pay their rent, then they'll need to stay off the Chairperson's radar in any negative capacity.

When it comes to good teaching, there are few substitutes for experience, and the Contingent possess that in abundance. I'd estimate that five years out of graduate school, they've taught twice as many courses, and maybe four times as many students as their tenure-track counterparts. Many of the non-tenurable, incidentally, *eventually* consider themselves teachers first and foremost. No longer distracted by the demand of having to write books or edit scholarly volumes, they can concentrate on students, if they so desire.

On the flip side, these instructors are often demoralized by their physical conditions of labor. True, they might not be required to publish. That doesn't mean, however, that they don't *want* to publish. Yet, how can they do that when they are laboring for ludicrous wages? What psychological calm can they achieve when they are denied any semblance of job security? The Contingent, I must mention, rarely have offices to meet students or hang their coats. They are often the recipients of tenured Fuddy Duddy condescension. Lord, are tenured Fuddy Duddies adept at making other people feel miserable.

All of this, as alluded to earlier, has an obvious impact on students. It's not optimal to have office hours with your professor on a bench in front of the library. It's not optimal when an instructor can't grade a paper carefully, because he spends his evenings driving an Uber. It's not optimal when faculty members simply disappear at the end of the semester. The high turnover rate of Contingent Professors is a perennial human resources conundrum. If the Contingent have advantages as teachers over the tenured—and I believe they might—then their poor working conditions serve to neutralize them.

When we leave the realm of my sketchy assumptions and turn to scholarly research on the subject, the findings are contradictory and inconclusive. One study conducted at Northwestern University posits that early exposure to non–tenure-track faculty correlates with students doing better in "subsequent coursework."[22] Conversely, other researchers posit that high exposure to Contingent faculty members may lead to lower retention rates (i.e., students staying within a program of study) among freshmen and sophomores.[23]

Investigators using completely different criteria infer that part-timers are less effective.[24] But as researchers dig a little deeper, an interesting finding comes to the fore. Some have argued that full-timers are more effective *whether they have tenure or not.*[25] In other words, these studies discern few differences between full-time Contingent and full-time Non-Contingent faculty members. This has not, I assure you, evaded the notice of the Board of Trustees.

It's part-timers, then, who are the pedagogical outliers; through no fault of their own, they represent a clear and present danger to student learning outcomes. An institution that serially subjects undergrads to exploited and mistreated part-timers may be crafting a recipe for pedagogical failure. All things equal, you want to attend a school *where undergraduates are frequently exposed to full-time professors*, be they Contingent or Non-Contingent. Herein lies the key to a positive Adjusted Strength of Faculty rating.

Maybe the full-time Contingents of the world perform capably precisely because they feel (somewhat) valued by the institution. Maybe it's because they are paid (just) enough to forestall starvation. Maybe the freedom from publishing lets them concentrate on pedagogy. Maybe they do better because they (usually) have a shared office space to park their recumbent bicycle in front of.[26]

This being said, I think it is important that we temper our relatively sanguine assessment of Contingent teaching prowess. Some non–tenure-line scholars might, on the whole, do a slightly more effective job of educating undergrads than tenure-line scholars. We should never lose sight, however, of how low we have set expectations. The Contingent likely teach better than the Non-Contingent *who really don't want to be teaching at all.* The Contingent, I remind you, received the exact same research-intensive/obsessive training in graduate school. Like all novice scholars, they dreamed of archives, not classrooms. My point is that no one gets into this business in order to teach.

***

Adjusted Strength of Faculty focuses our attention on an issue that Destination Colleges would rather leave obscured: the staffing of the American undergraduate classroom and the dodgy moral and economic considerations upon which it is based. It compels those headed to college to ponder the difference between a professor as a researcher and a professor as a teacher. Presently, those are two distinct, even mutually antagonistic, academic identities. Somewhere, some day, some visionary is going to have to figure out how to forge a generation of scholars who see research and teaching as an organic, divine unity.

Soon after Katelyn and Dylan's August arrival on campus, in a haze of heat and hope, they will be disabused of their illusions about their school's strength of faculty. Luckily, by the time they graduate, they'll stumble across a handful of truly committed teachers. In light of what we have discussed above, I don't think there's any logical way to predict whether those fine instructors will be tenured or Contingent, Fulls or Post-Docs. Under our current system, a great Scholar-Teacher is a sort of accident. His or her existence, to borrow a phrase from Joseph Conrad, is "an impenetrable mystery"—a phenomenon that somehow occurs *in spite of* graduate school training, our senseless tenure system, and the joyless Formula to which it is yoked.[27]

There's a reason, then, why undergraduates don't have the faintest clue as to the professional standing of whoever it is that's up there at the lectern. On the basis of what they encounter in class, Freeway Flyers and Fulls are usually indistinguishable. From the perspective of students, the rigid gradations of rank and status that are of supreme importance to professors have little relevance to their education. There is, then, a massive disconnect between scholarly hierarchies and student needs. Of what use is "distinguished faculty" to a sophomore if the faculty is so word-and-thought-defyingly distinguished that it can't be bothered to teach sophomores?

4

THE CAMPUS TOUR: TEACHING EXCELLENCE

Some backward-walking senior is giving you the campus tour. He exudes college pep and spirit the way a dog flicks off water upon bounding out of a river. This fellow is a repository of the oddest assortment of facts. President Warren Harding, he reports, delivered an address on these very steps. The new B-School building, on your left, is powered by geothermal energy. Every incoming freshman receives a complimentary iPad *and* a motorized golf cart.

This is all very intriguing, no doubt. But the guide does not—and cannot—address the issues that should be foremost among your concerns: What is unique about how this school educates undergraduates? What transpires in its classrooms? How do professors here enhance the career prospects of their young charges? Assuming an undergraduate has a "soul," how does this place make it possible for scholars to tend to, or mentor, that soul?

Challenging questions, every last one of them. Though I contend that for anyone selecting a college these are the questions that matter most. An undergraduate's intellectual, psychological, and, dare I say, spiritual growth is nourished by many things: by friends, by sports, by romance, by sexual experimentation, by parties, by tawdry-flavored vodkas, by internships, by community service, by the contemplation of the metaphysical, by the enjoyment of art, music, cinema, and by so much else. But ultimately, nothing will validate the massive investment of time and money that is a college education more than a student's encounter with professors.

I am speaking of those roughly 1,800 contact hours spent in the company of thirty to forty teachers. A young person's classroom engagement with a few dozen scholars across four or five years—more than anything else, *that* is what college is *about*. We scholars might be in a very bad way. We might be watching our way of life lurch into oblivion. We might, deservedly, be a class that history is about to roll. But until our countless detractors figure out a way to provide a better 1,800 hours, we remain the most important variable in a student's education.

All of this, naturally, is way above the pay grade of your twenty-one-year-old tour guide. Lurching toward oblivion? No one told him.

As for the college bound, when they visit campus it seldom dawns upon them to inquire about the aforementioned concerns. Which is providential because *no one on campus is capable of assisting them*. Most professors and administrators would be at a loss to provide answers—at least accurate or honest answers—to the queries above. Why this is the case is actually a pretty interesting story in its own right, and one I shall recount below.

So permit me to escort you on my own sort of campus tour. Consider this an unauthorized sounding into the mysterious depths of American undergraduate education. My task is to direct your gaze to essential aspects of college teaching that most schools would rather you did not see or could not show you, even if they tried.

The Saw Horse

Institutions of higher education love to brag about their "commitment to Teaching Excellence," or their "distinguished teacher-scholars," or their "inspired educators." But consumers beware: at best, these claims are aspirational. At worst, these are the effusions of PR specialists living at a remove from campus.

It's genuinely difficult for observers of Higher Ed—even those who are honest and non-partisan—to offer you any accurate insight about college teaching. There are many reasons for this, but none so formidable as the near total inaccessibility of the classroom. Outside of a matriculated student, *nobody* is in a good position to witness the commitment, or excellence, or inspiration of a college teacher.

Even professors rarely cross the threshold of a colleague's classroom. We are seldom invited to one another's lectures and seminars. We infrequently extend invitations. It goes without saying that an unannounced "pop-in" is strictly out of the question.

The door to a lecture hall could just as well be a police sawhorse—if that sawhorse stood behind a moat and was out-fitted with a rotating gun turret. Herein lies an unrecognized truth about American Higher Education: the inner workings of college teaching spaces are more or less unknown. What goes on in there? Line dancing? Capoeira? Face painting?

There are only two formal academic rites that beam a sliver of light into this deep ocean trench. The first goes by the name of "peer observation" or "peer rating."[1] The ritual features one professor coming to another's class to assess his or her teaching. The time and date of this event will be carefully negotiated in advance, as per institutional protocols. Documents will be signed and countersigned by the relevant parties.

Then, once a year or so, for about forty-five minutes, a higher-ranked colleague will "unobtrusively" pierce the perimeter, take a chair, and conduct an observation of a lower-ranked colleague (though for students the appearance of this outsider couldn't be more conspicuous if the observer came costumed as Death and rested his scythe on the radiator). Sometimes, especially when there is a heated interdepartmental squabble about the objectivity of the observer, two or three monitors will pile into the room—a veritable legion of doom.

Neither the observer(s), nor the observed, want any part of the observation process. Still, the exercise is deemed necessary by all college and university administrations. At Destination Colleges, a positive evaluation will have little effect on one's professional future. A so-so report will probably have no consequences either. A string of negative teaching reviews, however, can imperil the tenure prospects of an Assistant Professor with a weak publication record. As for a Contingent faculty member, a bad observation could terminate her employment altogether.

So, for three-quarters of an hour a year, everyone makes a good show of it. The observer(s) will feign interest, as well as the ability to competently assess pedagogical performance. The observed will dress spiffier, prepare better, and self-medicate more (or less, if necessary). The observed will then stage a meticulously planned, work of interactive theatre, which could be entitled *"Selfless, Supremely Competent, Super-Communicative, ME!"*

Outside of this yearly performance, we possess one other official mechanism for gauging instructional quality. These are the dreaded "Course Evaluations" or "Student Evaluations of Teachers" (SETS). Professors, be they Contingent or Non-Contingent, despise these things. During the last week of the semester, bleary-eyed scholars hand out standardized forms to stressed, overworked, and likely hung-over students. These forms have numerical prompts as well as sections for creative student input (e.g., "Sominex costs $5,000 less!").

A welter of research points to the deficiencies of SETS as survey tools. Some have found that course evaluations are beset by racial and gendered biases.[2] Non-response by delinquent undergraduates is a perennial source of distortion.[3] The physical attractiveness of the professor has been demonstrated to influence student assessments.[4] And no critique of course evaluations would be complete without drawing attention to the troubling fact that teachers who demand more from their students, grade harder, etc., will often be penalized for their commitment to the craft.[5] As two researchers recently put it: "teaching effectiveness, as measured by subsequent performance and career success, is *negatively* associated with SET scores" (italics in original).[6]

In any case, I have now exhausted the list of measurements that colleges and universities use to assess a professor's merits in the classroom. There's the annual staging of *ME!*, and the survey given in the last week of class. That's it. That's how individual teaching performance is gauged at most American institutions of higher education. Herein lies one reason why queries about instruction at the College of your dreams are so difficult, if not impossible, to answer.

In recent years, a new window into the classroom has emerged in the form of websites like ratemyprofessor.com and myprofessorsucks.com (though the latter no longer appears to be extant). Fuddy Duddies abhor those things even more than course evaluations. That's because these websites provide an accessible, public platform for anonymous student snark, shaming, and, for female faculty, sexism.[7]

Such sites, obviously, are for student use (and pleasure), not institutional use. The latter can never rely on ratemyprofessor. com in any official capacity for hiring and promotion decisions. The sampling is uncontrolled. Every imaginable form of distortion creeps in (e.g., students posting comments about classes they never took; professors posting as students, etc.). Moreover, there's an affluence of hyperbole on such sites (e.g., "The most brilliant professor at this school,"; "OMG, this person never blinks. #SerialKiller!!!").

And yet: since our classrooms are so roped off, and our measurement tools so afflicted by defects, these sites do offer some limited insight. The professor with 124 student reviews that concur: "doesn't leave enough time for classroom discussion," might acquaint himself with the concept of Q and A. The lecturer who gets dozens of "splooges her [fill-in-the-blank] ideology down everyone's throats" ought consider diversifying her syllabus so that other voices might be heard.

Multiple Metrics

There are, obviously, perfectly good reasons for keeping college classes inaccessible. There is, for starters, this quaint tradition called "academic freedom." In the Liberal Arts at least, that noble virtue would be endangered by an open-door policy in which any pretzel-munching shnook could glide into a class at any time. Such accessibility would likely impact how Humanists speak, reason, and argue in front of students.

Classroom inaccessibility, then, has a plausible rationale. This is why researchers have devised *many* other less obtrusive metrics that gauge whether college courses achieve their objectives, instill knowledge, smart up the youth, and so forth. Ironically, the sheer variety of tools they've fabricated makes the very notion of "Teaching Excellence" even more ambiguous. These tools must be considered very carefully by college-bound students and their parents.

We possess more metrics measuring effective college teaching than there are fraternities on probation in Florida. One scholar identified no less than *thirteen* different strategies that are used to assess instruction.[8] Some schools might rely on the self-reports of students. Other places might query the professors themselves, as a means of evaluating if a positive learning outcome was achieved.

More "scientific" alternatives are presently in vogue. The authors of the influential *Academically Adrift: Limited Learning on College Campuses* examine the scores undergraduates receive on standardized exams.[9] That test, known as the Collegiate Learning Assessment (CLA), was administered to students first in their freshman fall semester and, subsequently, in the sophomore spring semester. The inquiry yielded the unhappy conclusion that there is "no guarantee that undergraduate students are being appropriately challenged or exposed to educational experiences that will lead to academic growth throughout the wide range of diverse US colleges and universities."[10]

Among non-academics, a different way of evaluating teaching effectiveness has been devised. Philanthropists and politicians alike concur that good teachers and good schools produce gainfully employed citizens. Bill Gates opined that public education funding should be "well-correlated to areas that actually create jobs in the state—that create income for the state."[11] The Obama administration made much of tying federal support to how well a school's "graduates do in the workforce."[12] This initiative is not that different from repeated calls by Republicans to base higher education funding (and defunding) on how alumni fare in the labor market.[13]

My job is not to determine which measure is the best. I doubt whether such a determination is possible. Rather, I want prospective college-bound students to think about which measure provides them with the best *fit*. So, first let's imagine that an institution of higher education actually articulates its goals for educating students. Let's refer to this as a "coherent teaching philosophy." Not every place, obviously, will have the same philosophy. Some colleges might wish to craft employable, professionally polished graduates. Some might place a premium on analytical and writing skills. Some might want to form students who are fast, spry, and flexible thinkers.

Think of a tiny, Liberal Arts College situated at a comfortable distance from a major city. Half utopian colony, half regional hub for designer drugs, this anarchic school aims, above all, to foster self-esteem and confidence in its students. At such a place, it would be logical to assess students' *perceptions* of how much they learned. That would be the appropriate metric because it aligns with the culture of the institution. If internal research reveals that seniors feel they learned a whole lot across their four (or perhaps eight?) years, then such a place can claim that, by its own standards, they have achieved Teaching Excellence.

Now, let's think of a school of a less progressive bent. Its leaders believe that "self-esteem" is worthless psychobabble. What counts for them is performance, objectively measured on dry, grueling standardized tests. I have in mind certain military academies, or religious schools. At these, and other less touchy-feely places, no one would be troubled if wayward freshmen were occasionally "tased" with stun guns. The type of kid interested in such a school craves tough love, brutally honest feedback, and quantitative evaluations. The proper tool to measure Teaching Excellence here could be the CLA or professorial assessment of students.

Colleges and universities throw all sorts of "data points" about teaching at potential students. The job of the latter and their families is to discern if the data points indicate the type of school where they are likely to flourish.

Faculty-to-Student Ratio

Schools also tend to shock-and-awe potential customers with all sorts of dubious claims about how undergraduates engage with their professors. In the previous chapter, we investigated the questionable utility of "Strength of Faculty." We've just warned that boasts about Teaching Excellence are hard to substantiate either by personal observation or statistical measurement. Now, let's say a word about "faculty-to-student ratio"—a bullshit statistic if there ever was one.

In order to understand why this is so, we must first familiarize ourselves with a more meaningful indicator. I am referring to "class size," and I believe it to be among the most relevant predictors of whether a given school is truly committed to undergraduate education. What I am about to say, I say without apologies or excuses: in the Humanities and, most likely, in all of the Liberal Arts, smaller is better. Students learn more in small classroom settings. And they learn better. All things equal, the best colleges and universities are the ones that scale-down the rosters of as many undergraduate classes as possible.

If I and countless others are correct, then this is all very worrisome in light of a recent trend known as "massification." This refers to the staggering growth of class size witnessed over the past few decades.[14] During this period, schools have been forced "to accommodate greater numbers of students with less resources."[15] The logical dividend of this process is a large number of classes that have a large number of students sitting in them. Massification is particularly acute at public universities, where enrollments have swelled while government support has shrunk.

Researchers who study massification focus on everything from pre-calculus classes to macroeconomic offerings, to STEM disciplines, to writing programs.[16] Some scholars examine the relation between the number of pupils enrolled in a class and the grades they receive.[17] Others explore how class size impacts retention rates (i.e., whether a student who is massified, let's say, Freshmen year, is less likely to return to school by Junior year).[18] Still, others look at how undergrads seated amid a swarm perceive their own learning.[19] As with everything concerning the science of college teaching, the findings lend themselves to a myriad of measurements and interpretations.[20]

Encouragingly for those, like me, who view teeming enrollments as a threat to the Humanities, a *whole bunch of studies* suggest that massification has harmful effects.[21] One early (1990) investigation found that those who take large introductory courses receive lower grades in their subsequent classes than did those who take courses with fewer students.[22]

More recent inquiries have observed a negative and long-lasting relationship between large class size and student outcomes.[23] Scholars also call attention to the robust benefits that small classes have for a "variety of student populations, including underrepresented racial and ethnic groups, adult and reentry students, commuter students, female students, and international students."[24] Then there are the "higher order cognitive functions"—things like analytical reasoning and the ability to ponder things from multiple perspectives.[25] It's hard to impart these skills in learning environments that are too large.[26]

What, you may ask, constitutes "too large"? I would urge the reader to keep the number fifteen in mind. Most professors I have known concur that a course with ten to fifteen students is like the Golden Mean, or the sweet spot.[27] Researchers point to the figure of twenty-five as a sort of threshold. In other words, there is basically no difference in learning outcomes whether you have twenty-six, fifty-two, or 260 students.[28] After your roster surpasses twenty-five, it seems that "academic rigor and teaching quality" remain more or less the same no matter how many more bodies are added to the class.[29]

An undergraduate should not be serially "massified." High-priced colleges understand this well.[30] Why else do they relentlessly flaunt their Faculty/Student ratios, if not to foster an image of cozy pedagogical intimacy? Yet, FSR is misleading in ways obvious to anyone who understands the Big Lie of the American tenure system. If a school has 200 professors and 2,000 students, it will claim to have a FSR of 1 to 10. But this does not mean that every course has ten matriculated souls on the roster.

The tenure track and tenurable among those 200 professors might be teaching reduced loads. Or maybe they'll be on leave. Or maybe, as often happens, they'll be completely unaccounted for. If they teach at all, the tenured professors will mostly lead small seminars composed of upperclassmen or strictly graduate students. This skews FSR even more. It will also result in that sad staple of college life—high-density courses in freshman and sophomore year taught by harried tenure-track and Contingent professors. Thus, a school which advertises an FSR of 1:10 will nevertheless offer scads of massified introductory courses and required courses.

FSR is deceptive because it draws attention away from the infinitely more significant question of median class size. A better metric to ponder when considering a college is *what percentage of classes does the typical student take in which fifteen or fewer students are present*. If, hypothetically, a graduating senior will have spent thirty of her forty classes (i.e., 75 percent) toward the BA in such learning-friendly group settings, the preconditions for a very solid education are in place. Colleges vary in their average class size, but my vexed hunch is that at most places my 75 percent figure is turned on its head. Roughly three quarters of the undergraduate's class time is spent getting massified.

The Teaching Center/The Dean of Pedagogy

A college offering a high percentage of small classes is making a responsible decision. This school is wagering that all of its students will be better served by repeated, intensive, face-to-face, encounters with professors.

On the micro-level, this anti-massification policy has benefits for individual undergraduates. A class of fifteen or thereabouts, as we shall discuss later, is the gateway to meaningful student-professor relationships. It provides a platform through which scholars get to know undergraduates personally. If mentoring is ever going to occur, if souls are going to be tended to, then it's usually in these intimate settings where those relations begin.

Then again, it is important to recall that there is no *direct* correlation between small classes and effective teaching. Class size is one thing. Instructional competence is another.[31] Capping a class at a dozen or so undergraduates does not suspend the laws of gravity. In other words, de-massification alone won't turn quasi-catatonic Assistant Professors into classroom dynamos. Keeping enrollments at bay will not necessarily instill empathy in a Full Professor—the type of empathy that leads one to show up to office hours at 7:00 a.m. to accommodate a junior with a full-time job. Even if we chance upon a university that maintains civilized class sizes, the weak link will be the same as it ever was: a scholar who teaches poorly most likely because his or her concern is research, not undergraduates.

In an effort to remediate this perennial concern, some Destination Colleges create Teaching and Learning Institutes, or Centers for Teaching Excellence.[32] These units are tasked with improving campus pedagogy. Hundreds of such centers exist across the country.[33] Some are well-funded, state-of-the art programs like Harvard's Derek Bok Center for Teaching and Learning or Yale's Center for Teaching and Learning.[34] Others are ramshackle shelters; physical monuments honoring the concept of the afterthought.

If you are on a campus tour and your guide points out the TC, give it a good looking over. If no such visit is scheduled, then go off-roading and check it out on your own. I recommend this unusual course of action in deference to what just might be the Iron Law of American Academe: *space is truth, space is power*. There is nothing more revealing of a college or university's actual values and priorities than how it allocates space.

One effective way of gauging how seriously a school takes its Teaching Center is figuring out where the damn thing is located. Is it housed in the old tractor shed on the outskirts of campus? Does it reside in the well of the pool decommissioned since the $50 million Recreational Complex went up? Or has it been positioned in a set of suites adjacent to the commanding heights of the Provost's Office?

A more complicated task consists of figuring out if the Teaching Center has any real stature. Its staff (how many, by the way?) might send out a torrent of emails to the faculty with subject lines like "*Teaching Tip 142: The Wiki-Dickie*." But these messages might remain unopened and remanded to a scholar's trash bin. So, the question to bear in mind is: do scholars on campus fear and respect the TC?

As for respect, suffice it to say, humanists often do not generally hold the TC in high regard. Such institutes are often entrusted to scholars who received their doctorates in the field of Education. In my experience, these people are garden variety Fuddy Duddies. Yet, ancient disciplinary prejudices maintain that they are second-rate scholars. No PhD in Classics (languages mastered: ancient Greek and Latin; modern German, Italian, French) or Comparative Literature (languages mastered: modern Italian, German, Dutch, Spanish, French; familiarity with Hungarian) is ever going to genuflect to some Rando with a doctorate in Education who runs the TC. It's just not going to happen.

Most Humanists see the Professor of Education as a lightweight, confined to reading and writing in English (ha!) and conducting quantitative survey analysis (really?). Occasionally, a practitioner of a respectable discipline will direct the TC. To wit, a Philosopher or Art Historian who fell off the wagon somewhere along the way. Be that as it may, she or he won't get much deference either. Our guild does not tolerate apostasy.

Truth be told, many a scholar's day is devoted to goofing on the Teaching Center. Angela Sorby, a Marquette University English professor, had more fun doing precisely this than should be legal in most states of the Union. Writing in *The Chronicle of Higher Education*, Sorby lampoons the megalomania that sometimes characterizes the Professional College Teaching Pedagogue. She pens an imaginary memo from a Director of a Center for Teaching and Learning Excellence. "We at the CTL," avers the director, "spread excellence by steering faculty away from their focus on content (who, after all, needs to know the dates of the Civil War?) toward a more universal design model, in which knowledge-delivery systems are systematically delivered." The director's ultimate ambition is to supersize her unit from "a Center for Teaching and Learning" to "a Center for Teaching and Learning Teaching and Learning."[35]

We've answered to our satisfaction the question of whether Humanists respect the TC. This brings us to the subject of fear. Professors, at present, have little to fear. That's because these units do not possess the power of life and death; they can neither grant tenure nor snatch it away from a scholar's sinewy talons.

Most Teaching Centers serve in an "advisory" capacity. A scholar might go there to seek advice about glitches on the new teaching software she's testing out. In other instances, a Department Chair might suggest to an Assistant Professor that is scaring the children that he check in to the TC for rehabilitation. Upon his arrival, he'll receive counseling and maybe a few informational brochures. He won't receive any ultimatums. He won't be put on probation. That's because these units have little in the way of concrete, career-pulverizing, authority. Something must be done. But what can be done?

The Dean of Pedagogy

Teaching Centers, I believe, will always be ignored and disrespected, unless they strike terror in the hearts of Fuddy Duddies. In my view, the TC should be headed by a Dean of Pedagogy. Her powers would be immense—"dangerously uncircumscribed" complains the Faculty Senate.

Her job would be to scrutinize the classroom experience on her campus. She would articulate that coherent teaching philosophy alluded to earlier. When you come for your campus visit, it's her, the Dean of Pedagogy! who welcomes you and answers your questions (in her massive glass-walled conference room located in the President's Office). She speaks knowledgeably about Adjusted Strength of Faculty and class size. She defines what Teaching Excellence connotes around here. And guess who explains how it is measured? Yes, once again, that would be the Dean of Pedagogy.

Like all messianic figures, the Dean of Pedagogy is characterized by a troubling polarity. She retains a darker, more threatening side, especially as regards her interactions with the faculty. Sure, the Dean of Pedagogy would be all friendly on the outside. Sure, the Dean of Pedagogy employs all those goofy New Age teaching terms that PhDs in Education use and Humanists mock. But don't let the jargon and the little bowl of mints and gum she keeps outside her office fool you: in my reveries, the Dean of Pedagogy is authorized to completely fuck up your shit, by which I mean your tenure prospects or your reappointment.

Are you neglecting your classes? Do you spend your office hours hidden in a library study carrel munching on granola bars? Did you hand back your first graded assignment a week before class ended? Did you last read the novel you lectured on today around the time Bush invaded Iraq (and by this I mean H.W., naturally)? If so, the Dean of Pedagogy will take you *down*!

My Dean of Pedagogy, of course, is a figment of my imagination, an avenging angel who vindicates decades of undergraduate neglect. Like some ancient Near Eastern Goddess, her belt is threaded with the skulls of globetrotting scholars who schedule their final exams three weeks before the last day of class. One would be hard pressed, of course, to find such a person on the campus of any Destination College. But if ever a renaissance of college teaching is to occur, only a person with the superpowers mentioned above will be able to bring it about.

***

When you visit a college campus, you can see many amazing things. You can see the new Luxury Condo dorms inspired by the modernist aesthetic of Antoni Gaudí. You can see the seven varieties of quinoa in the cafeteria. You can see a life-size poster image of this year's recipient of the Distinguished Teacher's award (frozen in a dramatic pedagogical pose). But you can't see what the school authentically believes and actually does about undergraduate education. And when it comes to the monumental investment you are about to make—trust me on this—those beliefs and acts are far more impactful than the quinoa.

An informed college decision can only be made when those questions I drew to your attention above are asked. In all fairness, I am not sure that all of them can be answered. Certain things about teaching are just weirdly enigmatic. They will remain so at least until the advent of the Dean of Pedagogy. Later, I'll try to offer you some candid insight into what transpires between professors and students when they're working behind those armed sawhorses.

Still, the inherent mysteriousness of education does not excuse colleges and universities from providing visitors with as much accurate information as possible about those 1,800 hours. These schools deepen the mystery with websites that gloat about "Faculty-to-Student ratio," or link you to an article about a professor who just won a prestigious grant.

Were Destination Colleges to be honest about undergraduate education they'd talk about their Contingent labor force, massification, the unpreparedness of scholars for the demands of the classroom. And were critics of these schools to be honest about the root causes of these problems, they'd stop blaming professors alone. As we are about to see, there's plenty of blame to go around.

5

APPLYING TO THE RIGHT COLLEGES: A CHEAT SHEET FOR PARENTS

If my career spent in American Higher Education has endowed me with any wisdom to impart, then the wisdom would be this: *an undergraduate's encounter with professors is what really makes the difference in college*. I know this to be true. I also know that many scholars devalue this encounter, or fail to rise to its challenges.

Our failures have not gone unnoticed. Professors have earned the contempt of Culture Warriors, Silicon Valley Bros, Think Tankers, state legislatures, journalists, and others. These critics exult in kicking a little professor ass. Now, please don't misunderstand me: professor ass often wholly deserves to be kicked. Yet, we have come to that moment in our inquiry where it must be acknowledged that professors cannot be blamed for everything. We abide by the Rules of the Tenure Game—a game that never teaches us how to teach, and rarely rewards us for trying.

This is why some advance a counter theory of who is actually to blame for lackluster undergraduate instruction. The accused are known as "administrators." This wide-ranging term can refer to "professional staff" (generally lower-level support positions). But when professors pronounce the A-word with a snarl, we are really referring to those perched in the lofty managerial and executive suites. These seemingly omnipotent mid- to upper-echelon overlords include deans, provosts, presidents, executive vice presidents, and chancellors, among others.

The first thing an outsider needs to know about administrators is that there are a whole hell of a lot of them. The stunning growth of the academic support and managerial class is one of the most significant developments in the recent history of American Higher Education. From 1985 to 2005, full time faculty increased by 50 percent whereas administrative staffers ballooned by 240 percent.[1] One study shows that in 2012, there existed a staggering 456 employees per 1,000 students at private research universities.[2] Between 1987 and 2012, American colleges and universities expanded their administrations by more than *half a million* people.[3]

The second thing one needs to know about administrators is that professors blame them for every woe that afflicts American Higher education, and some woes that don't. Out of control tuition? That's because your school provides salaries for a jazillion associate deans and provosts. The dearth of tenure-track jobs? Well, our managers hire cheap, Contingent labor so they can afford to bring aboard more people like themselves. Cruddy classroom instruction? What else do you expect when you leave the running of the university to those spreadsheet reading, austerity-measures-implementing, redundancy-reducing, efficiency-enacting, commencement-ceremony-popping-up-out-of-nowhere, managerial motherfuckers?[4]

Critics of American Higher Education, as I noted above, tend to focus on the shortcomings of professors, not those who manage them. So do students—that's why we have websites like ratemyprofessor.com but not ratemyadministration.com. But what's undeniable is that *the administration*—not the faculty— makes the key decisions that result in how undergraduates are educated. The administration articulates "the vision," identifies the priorities, structures the budgets, and gives the faculty its marching orders. We disheveled Fuddy Duddies, holding our moistened towelettes at the white board, are but the dividend of those decisions.

Scholars tend to view admins as sellouts (many were once scholars themselves). I now share this opinion. Then again, administrators—with all of their power—*can* be a force for good. Competent leaders manage their faculty in ways that benefit student learning. So, to parents, guardians and college applicants, I say the following: if you wish to make an informed college choice, you need to understand what excellent administrations (I assume there may be a few left) do in order to optimize the aforementioned encounter between professors and undergraduates.

Cheat Sheet

A school with a fine teaching faculty (as opposed to a peck of talented phenoms) *never* happens by accident. It is the product of specific administrative policies. These policies are costly to implement. They are also very hard for outsiders to recognize.

Let me begin, then, by pointing to five measures implemented by institutions that wish to deliver a solid undergraduate education. Wherever possible I'll show you how to identify such initiatives as you shop for colleges.

Tip 1: The Formula. In previous chapters, I have spoken of "The Formula." This refers to the balance of Research, Teaching, and Service accomplishments that professors must demonstrate in order to gain tenure. At nearly all Destination Colleges, the Formula is heavily weighted toward scholarly research (between 70 percent and 90 percent of one's tenure decision is predicated on the quantity of one's peer-reviewed publications).

Institutions of Higher Education are reluctant to publicly state their Formula. This leaves those selecting a college at the mercy of promotional materials that rhapsodize about "Teaching Excellence" and "Our Dedicated Faculty." But why shouldn't those paying huge sums to attend a college know the true criteria upon which their teachers are selected?

A research-intensive Formula triggers a chain reaction that is catastrophic for professors and students alike. It virtually forces tenure-track professors to teach distractedly. Playing by The Rules Of The Game, they will move heaven and earth to shuck off classroom responsibilities altogether. The ensuing deficit of instructors leads administrations to stock up on Contingent faculty.

This results in the most devastating effect of them all. Permit me to posit an economic theorem: *paying tenure-track scholars a lot to teach a little directly results in paying non–tenure-track scholars a little to teach a lot.* Thoughtless administrations reason that Contingent faculty members should deliver an education to undergraduates. And then, even more thoughtlessly, they conclude that they should be compensated poorly for their efforts. A bad Formula, therefore, results in a situation that is ethically outrageous on about a dozen different levels: at many of the nation's leading (and most expensive) schools, the most valued professors conduct research while the least valued tend to undergraduates.

The broadest, most impactful change any administration can make is to *re-jigger its Formula in a manner that benefits its undergraduates*. A Liberal Arts College might grant tenure according to a 40/40/20 model. Forty percent of your promotion is based on your research, and forty percent on your teaching record (though the metrics to be used must be considered carefully; see Chapter Four). The remaining twenty percent is based on your service to the college community.

A religiously chartered school might calculate differently. It could place a premium on a scholar having received a doctorate from the perfect place. That could be a graduate program with an international reputation for excellence in certain sacred languages, or theological traditions. Yet, such a school might also see care of the student's Lutheran/Catholic/Nazarene/Mennonite soul as the single most tenurable quality a professor brings to the table. Ergo, this institution opts for a 20/60/20 arrangement.

What must be stressed is that a Formula can be configured in all sorts of ways—ways that match an institution's educational mission to its faculty and students. At present, Destination Colleges cling to a one-size-fits-all approach (i.e., tenure is achieved predominantly through research). This arrangement is murdering the Humanities, student learning, and, on the backstroke, the professoriate itself.

In recent years, critics have called for a pathway to tenure based mostly on teaching performance.[5] As we noted in Chapter Three, a cheaper version of this idea has already taken hold. Institutions are increasingly hiring Full-Time *non*–tenure-track professors to do the heavy lifting with undergraduates. I have yet to make up my mind on whether this shift is a good thing (it creates stable, better-paying jobs for more scholars), or a bad thing (it marks the Shock and Awe phase of the final destruction of the tenure system). I am, however, certain that it is preferable to the status quo: subjecting an undergraduate to a high proportion of inadequately paid, demoralized, itinerant, part-time professors.

Tip 2: Part Time vs. Full Time. This brings us to a less obscure criterion. Good administrations attempt to limit their students' contact hours with part-time faculty. Instead, they structure their Human Resources protocols so that the undergraduate is maximally exposed to tenure-line and Full-Time, non–tenure-line professors. Responsible managers make it highly likely that the person standing up there at the lectern is reasonably compensated, able to focus on teaching, and not living on Food Stamps.

It is possible to get a general sense of whether a school is committed to placing reasonably compensated instructors in front of students. To begin with, we have basic data about the professional composition of most American faculties.[6] In addition, the college shopper can simply go to a school's website—a treasure trove of useful information. Once there, locate the pages of, let's say, three or four departments of interest to you. Familiarize yourself with the faculty and start looking for patterns. What professors at what ranks are doing what? How are service courses staffed? Who is and who is not instructing undergraduates?

If 80 percent of the Linguistics Department is composed of adjunct Assistant Professors or the like, be afraid. If all the "Intro" sections in Psychology are taught by grad students or "TBA" (a euphemism for some underpaid, exploited rookie scholar), then take heed. If half the History Department is "on leave," then this is not the History Department for you. If Full Professors in English only teach advanced seminars (or graduate courses), consider applying elsewhere.

Tip 3: Small Classes. We've spoken about the merits of small classes. Administrations that value undergraduates keep their course sizes under control—a very expensive, but worthy, investment. I'd go as far as to say that not sitting in a bunch of massified classes, especially in Freshman year, might stand among the most important selection criteria for those making a wise college choice.[7]

Many schools post their course schedules on line, replete with figures showing how many students are enrolled in each class. A canny college shopper will identify the eight to twelve courses required for her major (those will be stipulated on the homepage of the department in question). From there, she should make a note of how many of those have less than fifteen students within. The more of these there are, the better. Conversely, if every single course for your major had thirty-five or more students last semester, a cost-benefit analysis is in order.

Tip 4: The Breach. Look for signs that professors and students interact meaningfully outside of the classroom. Later, I'll talk about the Wall of Separation that presently exists between them. At present, I simply wish to say that the opportunity / for a student to work individually with a professor must be reckoned as the Gold Standard of Higher Ed. Many places are increasingly creating programs in which students assist scholars with their research. Other initiatives draw undergraduates into collaboration on writing or performance projects.

There are many possible ways to breach the Wall. Schools, incidentally, love to advertise these "experiential learning" programs. No college website is complete without an image of a begoggled chemist steadying the arm of a begoggled sophomore as sulfur nitrate is dispensed from her pipette. I heartily endorse such initiatives, as long as there are many of them on campus and they are not created simply as photo ops.

Tip 5: Student-Positive Teaching Culture. In a similar vein, I admire places that facilitate casual interaction between undergraduates and faculty. An administration that encourages professors and students to play sports together, attend campus poetry readings, meet for informal lunches, and so forth, is creating real possibilities for undergraduate enrichment.

These are not kindnesses that scholars are inclined, by disposition or training, to extend. A good administration forges a culture of "teaching and mentorship." Professorial energies are redirected in ways that the professors themselves see as beneficial to their own careers and the well-being of their students.

I say this grimly aware that professorial delinquency is one of the largest and most unrecognized problems of the twenty-first century University. Simply put, scholars never appear to be around. It has been my personal observation that professors are living further and further away from their schools. I don't know how I'd go about proving this, but I'd wager that with each decade from the '70s forward, professors have dwelt, on average, five miles farther from their campuses.

Good administrations incentivize scholars to be around. They could provide reasonably priced housing, or programs that assure low-interest mortgage payments. They could set up bike racks, make parking free, and encourage Fuddy Duddies to join the gym at no charge. Maybe, in this way, the oft-heard student complaint that their professors are never in their offices, outside of office hours, might be alleviated.

Honors Colleges/Programs

It is generally assumed that large institutions, be they hulking Research Universities or gargantuan State Schools, never abide by the tips just discussed. That surmise is generally sound. There is, however, one significant exception to this rule. And the name of that exception is: the Honors College or Honors Program. In recent decades, institutions of this nature are increasingly being carved out from within gigantic establishments.

Often, these units come into existence because of frustration and despair. It all starts when a few professors, admins, alums, display road rage–like symptoms about the quality of undergraduate education on campus. Even the governor is pissed off; her son went to State and described his stay there as "like, uninspiring." The Office of Institutional Assessment commissions a longitudinal survey of 20,000 students that statistically validates the young man's concerns. The local media is fretting about a "brain drain"—Freshmen and Sophomores, feeling massified and anonymous, are decamping for other schools in other states. Something must be done! But what can be done?

Committees are convened. Town halls are staged. These concerns get batted around the Faculty Senate for about a quarter century or so (the pace of progress is slow in Academe). Then, there's a showdown and one faction on campus concusses another (nothing is achieved without violence in Academe).

The victors secure the budget needed to create a school within a school. An Honors College or Program is born!

There are upwards of a hundred or so of these in the United States. Their numbers are growing, especially at large public universities.[8] Throughout my career I have been involved with a few such ventures. Some of the most committed teachers, I have noticed, tend to gravitate to them. A properly administered Honors College/Program provides exceptionally good educational value for consumers. Further, these units often possess a war chest. In a bid to attract quality students, many will offer generous financial aid. In doing so, they poach talent away from elite schools whose formulae are full of toxins. Readers who wish to learn more can consult a work like John Willingham's 2014 cult classic, *A Review of Fifty Public University Honors Programs*.

I had a chance to observe one of the most well-known of these initiatives when I visited Arizona State University's Barrett Honors College. ASU has a national reputation as a hub for innovative thinking about Higher Education.[9] It is also very self-consciously a *public* university serving working and middle class students, many of whom are the first in their families to attend college. As you stroll around campus and marvel at the geological sight-gag that is a butte, you immediately recognize what a culturally and ethnically diverse state Arizona is.

Established in 1988, Barrett has upwards of 6,700 students with an average incoming GPA of 3.8, SAT scores of 1380, and ACTs of 29. I would characterize my meeting with its deans, Mark Jacobs and Peggy Nelson, as one in which there was remarkable agreement about what works and does not work in undergraduate education. This was unusual because "remarkable agreement" is not what typically ensues when I speak to colleagues about our pedagogy crisis.

In any case, the deans report that at Barrett, the Freshmen never sit in a course with more than twenty-one students, and the median is fifteen. While proper class size is commendable, I argued earlier that its benefits are achieved only when the instructors are competent. I asked the deans a question that any college shopper should pose: how does this school assure the presence of quality teachers in the classroom? They noted that when Barrett interviews prospective candidates, all conduct a teaching demo (with live students) *outside* of their field of specialization. Thus, the candidates are assigned a book to teach. This is an effective way to get scholars away from their "comfort zone." Once they are hired, these professors are expected to grow as teachers. To this end, Barrett assigns mentors (plural) to each new faculty member.

For their marquee gateway course, "The Human Event," the school employs forty-five Full-Time Contingent faculty members (thus no adjuncts, grad students, or Post-Docs teach the Gateway course). These instructors are hired on three-year *rolling* contracts. Once renewed, they have a cushion of thirty-six months of guaranteed employment ahead of them. Each instructor teaches a rather onerous 4-4. Though it's four recitations of the same course per semester, so preparations are kept to a minimum.

Barrett is an impressive place, managed and staffed by people who truly care about undergraduate education. My only concern is this: what's spectacular for the students might not be spectacular for the faculty. I'll return to this point later on, but we should note that the Barrett model has no-tenure. The tenured professors that honors students will meet will surface in the courses they take after Freshman year with the general population of ASU scholars. This is a conundrum for professors, but for students it is irrelevant. They receive personalized attention and solid instruction, all the while having at their disposal the massive resources of a ginormous Public University.

Get Your SLACS On

Just as it is misguided to assume that all large institutions do ignore undergraduate education, it is risky to presuppose that *all* Liberal Arts schools don't. Famous Liberal Arts Colleges (FLACs)—the ones that adorn Top 20 lists—in particular arouse my suspicions. As one faculty observer of Liberal Arts colleges points out, "those that are the most prestigious—have very high scholarly expectations, some of which would rival a lot of research universities."[10]

How did this come to pass? There is a lot of peer(-institution) pressure among Destination Colleges. Elite schools, no matter what their size, want to run with the big dogs. The cool kids in our industry lard their faculties with well-published micro-specialists from Top 5 grad programs. Succumbing to conformist impulses, many FLACs will do their best to keep up with the Joneses. We need, then, to be cautious about automatically equating a Liberal Arts college with heightened emphasis on teaching.

I have fewer concerns about Small Liberal Arts Colleges (SLACs). Everyone loves these schools. They are unassuming. They've often been around since the days of Ulysses S. Grant. Unless their Division III Athletic Director is caught smuggling elephant tusks, you rarely ever hear about them. Yet, when you visit a SLAC you are stunned by how deep and rich its local traditions are.[11] Unpretentious, tiny, low to the ground, located north of nowhere, locked in endless dialogue with townie yokels—it's really hard not to feel affection for these institutions.

A case in point is Albright College, located in Pennsylvania Dutch country. When I lectured there in 2015, I was surprised: 1) that it even existed and 2) at how robust its commitment to the arts was. I spoke to its then-president, Lex McMillan III, and came away with the impression of an administrator genuinely appreciative of, and devoted to, inspired teaching in the Humanities. That being said, Albright's challenge is the same that confronts all of us: college is expensive, and paying customers are far more interested in vocational, or "pre-professional," training than inspired teaching in the Humanities.

When I did some lecturing in 2016 at Hood College in Frederick, Maryland, I learned similar lessons. Its president, Andrea Chapdelaine, walked me through a postcard of a campus on a frosty spring day. She greeted everyone, from the gardeners to the physics professors, by name (civility in Academe: it always flabbergasts me). The classes I visited were perfectly sized and extremely well taught. The faculty I spoke to embraced their identity as educators, even though their research accomplishments were not inconsiderable. Yet Hood, like Albright, like so many small schools in America, must weigh its earnest commitment to the Humanities against the demands of consumers seeking financial return on their college investment.

Many SLACs live on the edge. Even a five percent reduction in the size of the freshman class can spell fiscal peril or even doom. These schools are constantly warding off disease and death. The threats force them to innovate in radical ways that belie their reputation as sleepy, bucolic backwaters. Their administrations are relentlessly creative and entrepreneurial in trying to keep their schools afloat. Hood, for example, has figured out how to build enrollment by appealing to transfer students and kids graduating from community colleges. The school also places an emphasis on the types of experiential learning programs discussed earlier.

SLACs with bad administrations—and there are many—will make the same stupid mistakes as mainstream schools. Or, different stupid mistakes. But those SLACs, like Hood and Albright, that play to their competitive advantages conform to at least four of the "best practices" I mentioned above. A student-positive Formula prevails. Undergraduates, obviously, are far less vulnerable to massification at these schools. Given how small (and isolated) these places often are, there exists every opportunity for undergraduates to forge meaningful relationships with their professors. The only question mark concerns whether students will spend a high percentage of their time in the classrooms of Full-Timers (one of the most difficult data points to track down).

***

I started this chapter by suggesting that administrations have a major role to play in the rehabilitation of American undergraduate instruction. Bear in mind, however, that—hyperbole being the coin of the realm—*every* administration will tell you that they are already doing this.

SLACs and FLACs, including religious, women's, and Historically Black colleges, often emphasize their commitment to teaching. In so doing, they sometimes imply, subtly or unsubtly, that others lack this commitment. Smith College, an illustrious school for women, declares on its website: "Many institutions talk about employing teacher-scholars, but not every college lives up to that ideal. Smith's faculty members are truly dedicated teachers and active researchers, performers and writers."[12] The insinuation that others misrepresent their true commitment to undergraduates is also evident in the following self-description of a women's college in North Carolina: "Many colleges say they offer a personal education. Meredith College delivers on that promise."[13]

Historically Black Colleges and Universities make claims of this nature, as well. Winston-Salem State University phrases it as follows: "Our faculty is known for their research expertise as well as their teaching in the classroom, where they have a long history of getting to know their students and working closely with them."[14] Then there are the religious colleges, many of which can be downright truculent about their competition. A lot of these faith-based institutions have a beef not only with traditional post-secondary education, but secular America as well. Christendom College, a traditionalist Catholic school in Virginia, declares: "We're not like other colleges. And that's a good thing."[15]

I find these invidious comparisons quite refreshing. I am enthusiastically *for* one sector of American Higher Education shit-talking another. Then again, I am troubled by an inconvenient fact. What vexes me is that the FLACs and SLACs just mentioned are recruiting their supposedly superior teachers *from precisely the same elite graduate schools that the research institutions are*. Let's reflect on that for a moment.

Few, if any, doctoral programs devote serious attention to training emerging professors in the art of undergraduate teaching. They sort of teach them how *not* to teach, if you get what

I am saying. All the PhD factories manufacture the same prod-uct: a micro-specialized researcher, possessing the interpersonal skills of a doorjamb, whose ability to instruct undergraduates is a complete unknown. There is no alternative pipeline. There is no "Indie Grad School Network" that breaks from the mold, and prepares scholars to educate others.

All the schools above boast about their superior teachers and their student-positive campus culture. They may be telling the truth for all I know. Yet, this raises a logical dilemma. Through what alchemy did they manage to take those micro-specialists out of graduate school and forge them into a cohort of com-mitted, conscientious, and skilled classroom teachers? The perennial challenge of applying to college is figuring out which schools actually have managed to effect this miraculous trans-formation on a large scale.

Professors, for their part, perennially complain about administrators. But only an administration can figure out how to turn scholars into Scholar-Teachers. Only an administration can force us to appreciate the unique value in our encounters with students. That's their prerogative and they've thus far failed pretty miserably, You can't blame professors for everything.

6

THE CRISIS OF STANDARDLESSNESS

"Crisis" is a word you tend to hear a lot these days in conversations about American Higher Education. There's a crisis of the Humanities—English majors are down, Business majors are up.[1] Rising tuition is a crisis of such magnitude that both Republicans and Democrats concur that government intervention is necessary.[2] Then there's college athletics run amuck, student alcoholism, pervasive violence against women on campus—crisis upon crisis.

The crisis I am about to examine is less well known and certainly less dire. But it has significant implications not only for professors, but for those trying to select a college wisely. I refer to it as the crisis of standardlessness. In the Liberal Arts, we are very, *very*, bad at making meaningful and accurate comparisons between this professor and that professor. We have the darndest time agreeing upon how we measure scholars against one another, even if they are in the exact same field and at the exact same stage of their careers.

Some might counter that this is a positive thing, a sign that we are all relatively equal, like members of a brainy commune. Perhaps, but American Academe is insanely stratified and *nothing like a commune*. Among professors, a handful of winners get tenure-line jobs at stellar schools. A few runners-up get tenure-line jobs at adequate or doleful places. The rest, or the overwhelming majority, are the tenure system's "losers" (i.e., Contingent faculty). When you look at which scholars end up where, there is nothing logical or fair about it either. The following scenarios should help illustrate these points.

Example One: Nowadays, it is not unusual to find a department where a bloated, Full Professor, age sixty-seven, has been out-published by a scrawny adjunct, age thirty-five. The adjunct did her apprenticeship in the late aughts. That was the era when it became evident to everyone that the "job market" was not about to pull out of its prolonged spiral dive. Unfortunately, it did not become evident to her.

In order to survive she, and so many clueless others, published obscene quantities of research. The gray beard, by contrast, received tenure decades ago when the "job market" was robust. Back in the seventies, one could get hired and promoted for flossing regularly. The older scholar makes about five times as much as the adjunct. Naturally, he teaches half as many classes.

Example Two: Professor Welch, over at Exquisite Boutique College, has been laboring for a quarter century on a "groundbreaking" study of late nineteenth-century Russian art. Colleagues like to recount tales of his epic labors, his devotion to craft, his personal sacrifices in pursuit of his subject matter.

Welch has not yet published his masterpiece ("my very own Fabergé Egg," he likes to joke). In fact, he hasn't published anything since the fall of the Iron Curtain that coincided with his being granted tenure. Rumor has it, though, that in five-to-seven years he'll turn in the final manuscript. As he hands it over to his editor, the Navy's Blue Angels flight demonstration squad will streak above him to commemorate this auspicious occasion.

Welch is revered in his field. Much more so than Boris, who teaches at a non-exquisite college and churns out about four, workmanlike peer-reviewed articles per decade. Welch sits on well-regarded editorial boards. Boris sits in his tiny, windowless, office double-checking his footnotes. Welch chairs steering committees for his professional scholarly association, The Nicholas II Society of Russian Arts and Letters. Boris chairs a Foreign Languages department whose forty-two instructors argue with one another for reasons that are nationalistic, ethnic, religious, personal, and sometimes completely incomprehensible. Welch is routinely consulted by nonprofits that dole out grant monies to humanists. But not humanists like Boris.

Example the Third: Two scholars were best friends in grad school. Both studied theoretical linguistics. They received the same training. They worked under the same doctoral adviser. They possess nearly identical publication records. They even both somehow showed up at the party celebrating their successful doctoral defenses in the same jeans with flared bell-bottoms from Cos! Yet, one teaches part-time at a community college and supplements her income doing data entry for an HMO provider. The other has a tenure-track job at an R1 university. Their relationship has grown strained.

Good scholars routinely end up at not good schools. Lesser scholars routinely end up at elite places. Many deserving scholars routinely find themselves trapped in dismal professional situations that are completely incommensurate with their achievements. Why is this standardlessness such an entrenched feature of scholarly life?

There are likely a dozen plausible answers to this question. In what follows, I'll limit myself to two explanations. Both of these hinge on the crisis we discussed earlier, the crisis of contingency. As usual, there will be plenty of administrative and professorial blame to go around. If you're currently drawing up a list of prestigious Dream Schools, you might want to follow this argument closely. Academic prestige, as we are about to see, is an awfully arbitrary thing.

The Blind Taste Test

Nowadays, being tenured or getting on the tenure track at any school in America is a sign of significant professional attainment. As you know, we refer to such people as "tenure-line faculty," and they comprise roughly 23 percent of the entire professorate.[3] Among this cohort, *where* a scholar works is a crucial marker of prestige and status. Thus, the Assistant Professor employed by an Ivy League school accrues greater glory than her counterpart at a Mid-Major. The latter, in turn, is more esteemed than a professor laboring at some far-flung SLAC. The same hierarchies prevail, I guess, among seventeen-year-old seniors comparing their college acceptance letters as they hotbox their parents' Toyota Priuses.

The juveniles and, distressingly, the professors are just following the logic of popular college ranking systems. They are assuming that the greater the renown of an institution as measured by *U.S. News & World Report*, the greater will be the quantity and quality of research produced by scholars in its employ. Is this correlation accurate?

If it were then it would follow that: an Assistant Professor in Anthropology at Princeton University (*U.S. News & World Report* 2024 rank #1) publishes more *and* better work than her exact counterpart at University of Southern California (*U.S. News & World Report* 2024 rank #27). The USC savant, in turn, outperforms the identically titled anthropologist at Syracuse University (*U.S. News & World Report* 2024 rank #73). The Syracuse ethnographer has a heftier CV than a comparable scholar employed at Oklahoma State University (*U.S. News & World Report* 2024 rank #196).[4] The better the university, the better the research its tenured professors produce. Right?

Well, Practice has a habit of trolling Theory. Let's imagine an experiment. All four of our hypothetical, tenure-track anthropologists are asked to submit an updated CV and all of their relevant publications. Upon the arrival of these materials, we scrub them of any identifying markers. The anonymous documents are then forwarded to a panel of experienced academicians, no-nonsense types who understand how the game is played. Their task: to figure out which CV corresponds to the sage employed at Destination College number 1, 27, 73, and 196.

All of our arbiters, I'm convinced, would fail this blind taste test. They would fail this test even if we asked them not to look at mere quantity of publications but quality as well. That's because the contestants would all look puzzlingly similar. It's quite possible that the judges would have assumed that the Assistant Professor at Syracuse worked at USC. And, yes, it is not unthinkable that they placed the Oklahoma State ethnographer in Princeton, New Jersey! The problem is not that the Princeton person is a slouch. The problem is that all four are publishing a lot and all are very impressive on paper. Ergo, it would, I submit, be impossible for the judges to distinguish between scholarly Coke and Pepsi.

Now, I would not deny that the distinctions among schools are a bit sharper at the rank of *Associate* and *Full* Professor. In other words, tenured senior faculty at elite schools often—*but definitely not always*—will have stronger publication records than their non-elite counterparts. We can't say for sure why this is the case. Do Senior Faculty members at leading colleges and universities publish more because of their genius and/or hard work? Or, is their success a result of having fewer teaching responsibilities and more administrative support for research?

But why should any of this be of interest to undergraduates? The truth is that they won't be seeing much of Associate Professors and even less of Fulls. Professorial prestige, we've been noting throughout this book, entitles one to teach *less*. This is why it's likely that more than half of a college student's encounters will be with *Contingent* professors, not Assistants, Associates or Fulls.

The college-bound should take heed: unless one is dealing with an exceptionally forward-minded Destination College, tenure-line professors and their dazzling CVs are a decoy; something a college can brag about prior to administering, so to speak, the old bait and switch.

The Spread of Contingency

As researchers, the credentials of nearly all Assistant Professors at schools ranked number 1 through 150 (and beyond) are strong and indistinguishable. Their skills as *teachers* are likely weak and indistinguishable (no one gets into this business in order to teach). Though, if I had to guess, I'd say the pedagogical edge probably goes to the scholars at 150. They will likely be subject to Formulae that incentivize them to pay attention to their students. Too, they'll have plenty of opportunities to improve their craft, even if they don't want to. They are contractually bound to teach 3-3s or even 4-4s. Over at the elite palaces, the requirement is a 2-2 or a 2-1.

But let's get back to our perplexing finding about research. How could it possibly be that the quantity and quality of publication is so similar? How could the standards for tenure-track professors be so out of proportion to institutional rankings?[5] The first answer to that question is the "job market."

American professors are confronted with an employment crisis the likes of which our guild has never previously encountered. There are plenty of jobs, mind you. The problem is that most of them are odious jobs when compared with what was once available. Just a few decades back, our tenure system was robust. Now, it lays dying.

Very many scholars in the Liberal Arts are trained at very good, very prestigious, graduate programs. Very few tenure-track jobs, or what scholars call "lines," exist for them to ply their wares. Study after study relays the grim news that tenure-track lines have been disappearing for decades.[6]

While lines are being cut dramatically, we have witnessed what one influential report calls the "spread of contingency."[7]

The phrase sounds reminiscent of something terrifying, like an outbreak of cholera or Bubonic plague. The metaphor is apt: as far as most professors are concerned, the contingency virus portends the extinction of our species.

The threat comes from our managers (i.e., administrators) who are committing to fewer tenure-track lines. The lines that they do authorize are designated for researchers who'll do some teaching on the backstroke. This leaves institutions with few resources to devote to the education of undergraduates. As the scholar Marc Bousquet observed in a landmark piece, "Under the actually existing system of academic work, the university clearly does not prefer the best or most experienced teachers, it prefers the cheapest teachers."[8]

Earning a doctorate in the Liberal Arts once entitled a person to a certain self-worth, a sense of honor, and usually a decent-paying job. It now entitles most scholars to become members of an "industrial reserve army" or a "surplus labor pool."[9] The collapsed "job market" results in a brutal asymmetry. A glut of qualified academicians applies for every available Full-Time job, and it makes little difference whether the post is at an Ivy League school or a community college.

Any scholar who sits on a hiring committee for a tenure-track professor knows this reality all too well. Hundreds apply for each advertised line. Of those hundreds, maybe fifty are quite good. Of those fifty, maybe ten are remarkable. Of those ten, often five are staggering in ways that make search committee members feel less confident about their own abilities. Which brings us to the cruelest statistic of all: of those hundreds, of those fifty, of those ten, of those five, *only one will be selected for the job*. Did the selection committee snag the best applicant? We'll address that shortly.

When a university appoints one of those Fine Fifty to a tenure-track position, this leaves forty-nine other qualified scholars desperately searching for employment. I estimate, generously, that in a given year there might be nine or ten tenure-track openings that are appropriate to each of the imagined anthropologists named above. So when application season ends, roughly forty of our Fine Fifty are left scrambling for Post-Docs, Contingent positions, and whatever dignity they can preserve.

They join a luckless procession stretching back at least a decade. Think of it this way: doctorates minted in 2017 will apply for an Assistant Professorship along with the ill-fated of the classes of 2016, 2015, 2011, 2008, and so forth. Their lives, hopes and dreams have been decimated by contingency.

The spread of contingency goes a long way in explaining the crisis of standards among professors. It also helps make sense of why our hypothetical blind-taste test yielded such baffling results. Our collapsed "job market" has resulted in a peculiar disconnect between the quality of an institution and the quality of its faculty. The lack of lines in the Humanities means that people with very similar—usually excellent—qualifications have fanned out at every imaginable post-secondary institution, from Ivies, to regional colleges, to community colleges.

Clever administrations at lower-profile schools have exploited this masterfully. Many have spent the past decades stockpiling blue-chip talents on the tenure line that previously might never have considered working at their institutions. It's a Buyer's Market. Perceptive speculators load up on bargains—and by bargains I mean scholars with significant research profiles who somehow have some semblance of teaching ability.

Job Searches: All Hail, The New Guy!

The academic "job market" is in tatters. As a result, every tenure-line position in the country attracts a surfeit of applicants. Among the finest of these candidates the differences in accomplishments, talent, and potential are small and subtle. In order to make the right decision, evaluators must marshal the diligence, focus, and cold impartiality necessary to tweeze out those fine distinctions.

The tweezing evaluators in question will almost always be Fuddy Duddies. Anywhere from three to twelve scholars will comprise the hiring committee. A departmental chair, or some other scholar/administrator hybrid will likely serve on the committee as well. Maybe a stray dean will represent the administration. But for the most part, longstanding conventions of faculty governance dictate that these searches are left almost exclusively to the discretion of professors.

Which is, perhaps, why academic searches provide us with so much rich comic earth to frack. Even when the job market was stable, in the once-upon-a-time era of the non-disrupted Academy, our hiring protocols left much to be desired. Now, more qualified candidates than ever before vie for our attention. We stand, as always, unready, unwilling, and unable to properly assess their prodigious talents. The crisis of contingency is largely the fault of administrators. The crisis of standardlessness, however, has a lot to do with the dysfunction of scholars.

A comparison with another industry may provide some useful context. The National Football League conducts its annual draft in the spring. The proceedings are splashily broadcast to the multitudes. Viewers are mesmerized by eye-lacerating graphics, torrents of analyses, and endless clips of very large men pulverizing other very large men.

Prior to all that sound and fury, thirty-two professional franchises spend the fall and winter studying thousands of college athletes. The work is entrusted to well-staffed scouting departments who sojourn to gridirons across our nation. Ever eager for comprehensive data, the evaluators consult with leather-lunged college coaches, coked-up assistants, and shifty athletic directors. After that, the scouts hunker down in dark film rooms pouring over infinite reels of tape. All the better to pinpoint the precise merits and demerits of the players they vet.

The prospects are graded according to rigorous criteria and then reassessed, in person, at a Combine. At this event, even more observers, including hundreds of sports journalists, join the scouts and front-office people. Security and background checks are performed on the athletes. Intelligence and psychological evaluations are administered. The process spans months and costs each team millions of dollars. And even with all of that effort, all of that labor and industry, football teams make mistakes—often referred to as "busts"—on a regular basis.

Our drafts are somewhat different. Except for the whole part about "busts" and making mistakes regularly. Which is unfortunate because a person hired to a tenure-track job is not expendable like a Nose Tackle selected from McNeese State. Our busts can conceivably hang around the "team" for half a century or so!

The NFL's draft occurs every year. Conversely, no one quite knows when an academic job search might take place. And yet, a tenure-track line is a multimillion-dollar investment. It obliges the institution to guarantee a scholar's salary for, potentially, decades. The decision to grant a line to a department and activate a job search rests with deans and provosts and presidents. Their ways are inscrutable.

If your department does get the nod then: euphoria. A collective delirium takes hold. Everyone reasons that the New Guy, whoever she or he might be, will balm a thousand wounds, redress an infinity of injustices, and generally set things right. The New Guy'll teach the Intro class (which no one wants to teach and has gone untaught for three years). The New Guy'll run the unstaffable capstone seminar that meets Friday at 4:00 p.m. New Guy'll coordinate and oversee the twenty-three members of our Contingent staff. Who knows, maybe New Guy will be cute or a quick wit—we haven't had a good laugh here since the global financial meltdown of 2008. Come to think of it, we haven't had a line since then either. Yes, we're going to like New Guy!

Then an ad is posted, and an entire *civilization* of wannabe New Guys comes calling. Some of their applications arrive the day the ad went up. A few, inexplicably, show up the day before. Still others come in outsized boxes delivered on hand trucks by courier services. I confess to having a soft spot for the letters that materialize weeks after the deadline. Those are always accompanied by a "human interest" story. ("*From the outset, permit me to apologize for the late delivery of these materials. While researching my forthcoming monograph in Vitebsk, Belarus, I was detained and incarcerated by local authorities who the State Department now informs me…*")

With the "job market" in disarray, every posted tenure-track opening yields a deluge of applications, a blizzard, a derecho, a tsunami—you can supply your own metaphor as long as it archly conveys that a natural disaster is taking place. The whole selection process is a catastrophe, not only for those evaluated (see below) but also for the evaluators themselves.

Football teams employ squadrons of well-paid scouts whose sole task in this life is to vet potential draftees. Colleges, by contrast, entrust that mission to stressed-out, overworked tenure-line professors. They are never compensated for serving on a search committee (or any committee). The process is reckoned as "Service." Universities get what they pay for.

In pursuit of New Guy, professors will be confronted with hundreds of applications, three times as many letters of recommendation, and enough offprints of scholarly articles to fill the Library of Congress. By my estimate, the committee members will scrutinize each CV for about two to five minutes. Besieged by a surfeit of credentials, the typical harried evaluator will focus on two vital metrics: 1) where a scholar received the doctorate and 2) what the scholar has published. That takes about ninety seconds. In the remaining ninety seconds, assuming the applicant has not been consigned to the thickening Reject Pile, the reviewer glances at what courses the applicant can teach. So much for pinpointing precise merits and demerits! And it goes without saying that no psychological evaluations are ever administered.

The search is kicking into high gear. Timeless irregularities of academic culture begin to infest the process. For starters, scholars tend to hire "tribally," preferring people with similar intellectual interests. Politics and ideology also rear their scowling heads. The radical Left is notorious for commandeering search committees. That's why some Film departments are staffed solely by Deleuzian Maoists or Vegan Derridaians. Sometimes, professors look exclusively for people who attended their own graduate schools. How many departments have I seen with a cancer-cluster of hires who received their doctorates from the same place, under the same doctoral adviser?

In accordance with these peculiar criteria, roughly 95 percent of the aspirants will soon be eliminated. The field has been narrowed to three or four outstanding individuals (though that decision is always contested and accompanied by a few resignations from the committee expressed in 10,000-word manifestos). Once the short list is drawn up, rituals of backchanneling, influence-peddling, and whoremongering ensue that would impel a K Street lobbyist to find Christ. On-campus interviews are booked. Rumors run rampant. Unexpected alliances crystallize around unexpected candidates.

Cross-cutting through all of this intrigue are other distractions. Scholars have the ill-advised tendency to fall in love with one another. Their passion gives rise to an "academic couple"—perhaps the most dreaded phrase in a search committee's lexicon. No search, it seems, is complete without this ghastly spousal subplot. It comes out of nowhere—like the toothy maw of the monster from *Jaws* emerging from the sullen deep—and drags the entire process down into some dark, litigious murk. Sometimes, the selected candidate won't come unless her partner (referred to as "the trailing spouse") is given a professorship as well. If you've ever sat in a college class and been utterly mystified as to *why* your professor is even at this institution, I have a handy rule of thumb: because he's some famous professor's husband, that's why!

Ought I mention "inside candidates"? The darkest secret of the tenure-track search is that its outcome is fairly often foreordained. A tenure-track line is a precious commodity—the academic equivalent of a city winning a bid to host the Olympics or the World Cup. Is there any wonder that the desire to attain this treasure trumps our ethical impulses?

I regret to report that in more than a few cases the job description, the composition of the committee, the questions asked at the interview—all of it has been rigged to assure that one predetermined candidate is hired. That lucky soul could be a trailing spouse, a Visiting Professor that everyone adores, or some star at another institution.

Need I point out that for the poor applicants, the entire ritual I am describing is time consuming and expensive? Rebecca Schuman, a critic of Higher Education writing in *Slate*, has chronicled this well. She reminds us that a job seeker in academe actually has another job: and that job consists of applying for jobs.[10] The ritual is also needlessly degrading.

That a process such as the one I am describing rarely conduces to positive outcomes for employer and employees is overdetermined. In the NFL, General Managers with a bad record of drafting are almost always fired. The scouting departments go down in flames with them. In Higher Education, there is no comparable form of accountability. We never look back from a distance of, let's say eight years, and ask if the committee made the right choice. No school has the time, or resources, or will to conduct such an inquiry.

Those audits are only conducted in the minds of irate scholars, the ones who were rejected. They labor bitterly at some lesser place, an unamiable place. That they have outperformed the person who was selected for the job they coveted is only a minor consolation.

***

Ironically, the professorate's misfortune (and incompetence) is a boon for college consumers. If you select a college on the basis of professors with formidable research profiles, then here's some really good news! There are some phenomenally well-credentialed scholars at the 150th-ranked school in America. Truth be told, there are phenomenal scholars at schools ranked a few hundred slots lower than that.

But you're not selecting a college on the basis of professors with formidable research profiles, are you? I mean, I sincerely hope you're not. What does it matter to you if your professor has a monograph with prestigious Oxford University Press as opposed to slightly less prestigious Routledge Press? Why should you care if your Econ teacher has published eleven or nine articles in "Top 5" journals? If a Psychology professor has a Google Citation Index of 2865, does that render her more valuable to your education than another scholar whose work has been referenced 1725 times?

You shouldn't care about any of these things half as much as whether your professor can help you learn (yet another metric whereby school 150 overachieves). This reminds us that the standards that are relevant to professors and administrations exist in a tragic tension with the standards for properly educating undergraduates. Our tenure system cross-fertilized with our collapsed "job market" and then mated with Fuddy Duddy dysfunction has resulted in some very peculiar standards. On the basis of research alone, the less prestigious schools are not that far behind the most prestigious ones. On the basis of teaching alone, the former likely outperform the latter.

7

THE BEST COLLEGE TEACHERS: DON'T BELIEVE THE HYPE

Each year, the journal *Literary Review* bestows the Bad Sex in Fiction Award upon an author who produces coital-themed prose of exceptionally poor quality.[1] We professors ought to adapt this idea and honor the Most Unrealistic Depiction of a College Class in American Cinema. My nomination, hands down, goes to the 2003 *Mona Lisa Smile* starring Julia Roberts. The actress plays Professor Katherine Ann Watson, an Art History instructor teaching on a one-year contract at Wellesley College in 1953.

There is so much that is askew in *Mona Lisa Smile*'s classroom scenes that I don't even know where to start. How do we account for students who have memorized the entire textbook by the first day of class? How could a bunch of twenty-year-olds know enough about scholarly mores to condescend to Professor Watson for not yet having her doctorate? And what's with that administrator who lurks in the back of the hall observing Professor Watson's first lecture? Who is that guy? Doesn't he realize that his presence violates every norm of academic freedom (see Chapter Four)?

I'm also confused as to why, by movie's end, each student presents the professor with a well-executed painting of flowers. I mean, I get the allusion to their burgeoning, agentive, feminist consciousness and all. But when did History of Art 100 morph into a studio class?

Not everyone at Wellesley offers heartfelt gifts to the freewheeling Professor Watson. The administration renews her contract only on the condition that she tone down all the liberal stuff in her lectures and personal life. (Here's a scholar who could really have used the protections of tenure!) Professor Watson refuses to compromise her integrity and moves on. Upon her bittersweet departure, crestfallen students escort her taxi past the campus gate on their bicycles. As they complete their rolling salute to pedagogical greatness, they tear up over the loss of an instructor that Makes Us Think. And Love.

The question for me is not why a Hollywood depiction of college life is so off the mark. We Humanists—who struggle to create a shoebox diorama—ought not cast aspersions on the artists who produced a movie as pretty as *Mona Lisa Smile*. No, the question for me is why do narratives about Great Teachers abound in hype and sentimentality.

This tendency is certainly not restricted to cinema. Even serious academic studies of pedagogy traffic in this sort of hyperbole. I think of Ken Bain's 2004 *What the Best Colleges Teachers Do*. This thorough and well-intentioned study set out "to capture the collective scholarship of some of the best teachers in the United States, to record not just what they do but also

111

how they think, and most of all, to begin to conceptualize their practices."[2]

Bain, admirably, deploys multiple metrics to identify the Best Teachers. His research abides by rules of rigorous scholarly inquiry. Yet, even this trained academic can't avoid excessive praise. "How does Ann Woodworth, a professor of theater at Northwestern University," asks Bain, "lift her acting students to heights of thespian brilliance?"[3]

Harvard Professor Michael Sandel, teaching a 700-person class (!), is commended extensively. According to Bain, he helps his students become "good political philosophers" by asking them to imagine "fundamental issues of justice and understand their own thinking."[4] Bain is equally unconcerned about massi-fication when he lauds another Best Teacher for asking pre-class questions of his 200 registered students.[5]

Although Bain concedes that even the best instructors have bad days, his analysis loses sight of this truism.[6] The educators he writes about appear to consistently elicit epiphanies in their students. These scholars are rarely shown to stumble during a lecture or mess up. They never arrive late for class or lose their temper with insolent seniors. Grade disputes (otherwise known as "grade-grubbing"), a recurring type-scene of any college teacher doing his or her own marking, are nonexistent. The students themselves play but a supporting role in Bain's analysis. They exist as fans. An audience. Reaction shots.

As part of my ongoing crusade to narrow the gap between what is said and what is done in Higher Ed, I'd like to advance a grittier assessment of good college teaching. In order to do so, I must first provide you with some clear-eyed perspective about how undergraduates and professors *actually* engage with one another today. Once we do that, we'll be able to decommission some misconceptions about "Best Teachers." I hope the forth-coming will spur students, be they current or prospective, to reconsider what makes an instructor special.

Cordial Estrangement

If we want to have a frank discussion about college teaching in the twenty-first century, we must come to grips with the fact that the twentieth century is over. This means that we should de-sentimentalize the encounter between the student and professor.

Some imagine a college campus as an isolated ecosystem in which scholars and eighteen to twenty-two-year-olds—everyone finishes in four years right?—exist in a symbiotic relationship. The professors, in this pastoral, dwell in weathered, but comfortable detached homes just a stone's throw from campus. They pass their days in their departmental offices, where they counsel their students, and read scholarly papers as they fiddle with the kindling in their pipes.

Undergraduates routinely visit them, alighting from their study carrels, lecture notes in hand. The students ask their professor follow-up questions about yesterday's class on the great German sociologist Max Weber. They report their professor's (detailed) answers to their roommates during late night bull sessions in the dorms. Sometimes a heated argument breaks out among the assembled underclassmen. They debate what Weber really meant when he spoke of "the disenchantment of the world." Finally, at 4:00 a.m., a truce is reached: they all resolve to drop in on their professor tomorrow so that he might adjudicate their disagreement.

On this imagined campus there's a welter of student-teacher engagement. Ms. Meyers (no matter what your professorial rank may be, we refer to you as Mr. or Ms. around here) is what is known as a "Den Mother." Students, particularly young women, flock to her office or home to talk about academic and non-academic concerns. As for her husband Mr. Meyers, the chair of Comp Lit, why, he's a live one! He likes to throw raucous parties at the beginning of every semester where he's been known to crack out his bagpipes. Rumor has it that he's wont to act inappropriately when he's thrown back a few G and Ts. Some whisper that he once had an affair with a senior by the name of Sally a few years back.

Few scholarly books could do more to disabuse a reader of the hallucination just presented than *My Freshman Year: What a Professor Learned by Becoming a Student.*[7] This excellent study was published in 2005 by an anthropologist writing under the pen name Rebekah Nathan. For any scholar, the premise of *My Freshman Year* is the stuff of night terrors. The book's author, a tenured fifty-two-year-old ethnographer, matriculates, undercover, as a student in the college *at which she teaches.* She even takes up residence in the dorms. This feat of derring-do reminds us that anthropologists are Higher Education's last remaining daredevils, stuntpersons who will launch themselves off a 13,000 foot cliff in a wingsuit in pursuit of Knowledge(s).[8]

One incontrovertible conclusion to draw from the book is that undergraduates are busy and distracted. They are cross-pressured by jobs, by club activities, by internships, by romance, by social obligations, by other classes. Put simply, students have a lot going on in their lives—and not much of it has to do with us. As Nathan notes: "Most professors and administrators overestimate the role that academics plays in student culture, and as a result they magnify the impact of teachers and classes on student life and decisions."[9]

So in lieu of that follow-up visit to gain greater insight into Weber, a student today is much more likely to be working in order to pay for that class on Weber (or, more likely, a class on Management and Organizational Behavior). A recent analysis argues that college students spend significantly *less* time studying than do high school students (10.9 fewer hours per week).[10] The daily commitment to educational and work-related activities is about equal.[11] In terms of long-term fifty-year trends, full-time students are spending less and less time preparing for class.[12]

Nathan raises a concern that speaks to the reality of contemporary professor-student relations. "As an anthropologist," she laments, "I was humbled to see how little I, as a professor, knew of my students' academic world."[13] Earlier, we saw that the converse of this observation is equally true: students have no idea who we are. This mutual ignorance is crucial for understanding the context within which we educate undergraduates. For the bitter and undeniable truth is that professors and students in twenty-first century America are cordially estranged.

The two groups lead parallel lives on campus. Their only point of intersection being the occasional classroom spaces they happen to inhabit concurrently. As far as a Professor is concerned, the students arrayed in front of him could just as well be a flash mob that assembles twice a week and takes notes. Professors and students do not necessarily think ill of one another. The truth is that they hardly think of one another at all.

What has been lost, in both theory and in practice, is the idea of meaningful and sustained relations between faculty and those they teach. Classes, as we are about to see, proceed in an instrumental manner. Office hours are perfunctory, and the students who do attend only come to discuss finals or to rehearse excuses for late papers.

Mentoring (see Chapter 8) has become a lost art form, like the jump shot or designing album covers. Nathan homes in on an essential truth when she sighs: "There is no doubt that special professors do make a difference in the life of specific students, but overall, I'd suggest, student-teacher relationships play a relatively minor role in the experience of undergraduate life in a large university."[14] As far as I can tell, nearly everyone, from undergraduates, to professors, to administrators is at peace with this arrangement—an arrangement, as we shall see, that has significant implications for how we work in classrooms.

How did it come to this? What happened to the collegiate ecosystem described/imagined above? Why does it only persevere at a few colleges today?

The developments that resulted in cordial estrangement are complex, and I certainly can't pinpoint them here. My passing conjecture is that things started shifting around the 1980s. Maybe it was the increasing emphasis on research over teaching that drove scholars away from discussing Max Weber with their undergraduates. Maybe housing prices rose, and it became more difficult for professors like the Meyers to purchase properties near campus. Maybe the spread of Contingency reduced the faculty's available time.

Maybe it was the expansion of the administrative class that inserted itself as a firewall between professors and students. Maybe economic trends forced more kids out of their study carrels and into low-paying jobs. Or maybe—and we'll have more to say about this in Chapter Nine—a growing monitoring of sexual harassment decreased student-professor proximity; predators like Mr. Meyers, after all, were not entirely fictional.

The Transaction

It's been two decades since Nathan performed her fieldwork. Speaking from experience, the context in which professors and students interact is no less transactional. Professors continue to teach classes because they have to in order to get paid and/or get to their research. Students continue to take classes in order to receive concrete deliverables. They need to fulfill a specific requirement toward their degree. They need to receive a grade.

On the first day of school, veteran teachers are never surprised to learn that many undergraduates have no idea who their professor is or what the class is even about. The kids registered because the course knocked out a prerequisite. Also, it didn't conflict with their internship or shift at the coffee shop. This is a course on Death and Dying in Russian Literature? Really? Sounds like a lot of fun. Let's do this!

True, undergrads might select a class because they hear solid buzz about a teacher. Though that buzz likely entails that the professor: 1) doesn't assign much work, 2) doesn't take attendance, and 3) is an easy grader. If the professor has a reputation for saying and doing fun stuff in class, that's appreciated, but by no means essential to a student's scheduling priorities. In Chapter Two, we saw that students rarely know their instructor's professional rank. It's not surprising, then, that they often don't know their professor's names—even by semester's end. Professors rarely take umbrage—they probably don't know most of their students' names either. This is cordial estrangement in action.

The transactional arrangement I am describing isn't ideal. But it is the hand we college educators are dealt. Committed professors don't pretend that it's 1953. They see and respect students for the busy, overworked, distracted souls that they are. We want to un-distract them, naturally. The prose of Hawthorne, we know, has more to offer them than their stupid internship. The quirky social theory of the German sociologist Georg Simmel beats serving coffee any day. So, good teachers craftily exploit all the possibilities that the transaction offers. We do it to honor Hawthorne and Simmel. We do it because we feel these thinkers have something priceless to offer these kids.

Besides, what is a transaction, anyway, but a convergence of wants? Here's what I want. I want my students to learn how to read texts carefully. I want them to come to every single class prepared to speak eloquently about the literature we are reading. I want them to engage with other students and—this is very important—to listen to them as well. I want them to write about their ideas in lucid, convincing, vivid prose. And, I'm just going to be honest here: I want the materials we read and discuss in class *to aggressively infiltrate their little fucking brains*. Let them read Hawthorne's 1836 "The Minister's Black Veil" and have nightmares.[15] Let them read Simmel's 1908 essay "The Stranger" and have his insights about romantic love poison every subsequent amorous encounter they ever have.[16] Those texts sure did that for me!

Thank the Lord, I have one thing students want: they want good grades. Aside from a few idiosyncratic undergrads, the grade is always the carrot and the stick. The grade is the engine of the transaction. The grade is where what I want aligns with what a student wants.

Now I'll be the first to concede that "quid pro quo" lacks a certain magnanimity. Then again, quid pro quo is about as sturdy a driver of human accomplishment as any I know. For these reasons, I appreciate a professor who manipulates the transaction in a way that virtually forces students to immerse themselves in Hawthorne and Simmel. Sure, students are being lightly coerced—but it will be good for them, those little bastards.

Good college teaching, I have insisted, triggers thoughtfulness in students. Yet, it is often forgotten how much banal, labor-intensive work a professor must perform to make that outcome possible. It all starts with a well thought out, demanding syllabus. That document is at once a schedule and a constitution. It informs students of exactly what is expected of them. *Half the challenge of teaching a good class is spending countless hours architecting a keen syllabus.*

Apathetic teachers hate this, not only because it is so time consuming but also because it obliges them to a semester's worth of deadlines and commitments. Therefore, you should be suspicious of professors queued up at the departmental copying machine printing their syllabi on the first day of school. You show me a professor who hasn't thought through the syllabus, and I'll show you a class that is invariably going to suck.

Syllabus design is just one of those many unriveting components of effective college instruction. There are other unriveting components—stuff that you would never include in a movie. I have nothing but respect for those scholars who return exams and papers promptly (punctuality has never been our strong suit). My colleagues who provide detailed written and oral feedback are doing holy work. It might sound like pop psychology, but students need to know that you notice them, recognize them, are thinking about what they do. Convince them that you are acutely aware of their progress, or lack thereof, and they *will* come by your office. Maybe they'll even discuss the disenchantment of the world with you.

This is why a professor lecturing *at* 700 students should never be compared to one teaching twenty-five. Can 700 people ask questions in class? Can 700 people come to office hours? Can any one instructor learn the names of 700 human beings, twenty-two of which will be named Alex? Can any one instructor monitor the progress of 700 people?

The large (and even small) lecture hall is nowadays often the site of an unspoken student-professor conspiracy. Many professors want to focus on research and get their teaching over with. As a result, they don't demand too much of students. Lectures will be minimally planned, which is why they so often drift and dawdle. Grading will be infrequent, soft, and thoughtless. When student evaluations are distributed at semester's end, students will tip a professor who abides by the rules of the transaction (and, yes, studies show that professors who demand less and give higher grades score better on student evaluations).[17]

My appeal to students is to recognize that professors who game the transaction this way are not good teachers, *no matter how knowledgeable and/or entertaining they might be*. Remember, it's easy for a professor to skim your essay, to scribble a few illegible comments on it, to sleepwalk through a lecture, to overlook your many grammatical infelicities and your appalling failures of logic. The system is set up for professors to not care about you. And, ironically, it punishes those who do.

What's Wrong with the Best Teacher?

Can I be perfectly frank with you? The whole discourse of Best College Teachers strikes me as bullshit. Whether it's Baylor University's Robert Foster Cherry Award for Great Teaching (with a cash prize of $250,000), or those "Faculty of the Year" honors that are dispensed at every college according to performances that are, literally, inscrutable—it all seems off to me.[18] I don't doubt that there are some truly phenomenal teachers out there who have deserved these accolades (just as I don't doubt some duds have received them as well). Yet, this system of tribute undermines a lot of what we aim for as educators.

To begin, these types of prizes draw attention away from the fact that educating an undergraduate is a *collective*, not an individual, enterprise. The type of knowledge we impart in college is sequential. It is pointless to take a specialized course on the Sociology of Pierre Bourdieu before you've taken Intro to Sociology, and Stratification and Social Theory, and Cultural Sociology. The concept of an academic major implies the existence of a reasonably well-ordered curriculum. One great teacher cannot teach an entire curriculum. That takes a team.

I once had a colleague who taught a 200-level class. She genuinely loathed the fellow who taught the 100-level that was a prerequisite for her own. The latter was a campus legend. He was a flamboyant character who gyrated and twerked as he lectured. By the time his students cycled into her class, they knew exceedingly little about the subject matter. Her 200 regressed into a 100, because the guy in the 100 was teaching—well, she had no idea what he was teaching. He did win many Faculty of the Year awards though.

The team metaphor reminds me of another thing that irks me about Best Teacher banter. Individuals on teams have different skills and strengths. Yet, conversations about great instructors never seem to recognize that professors are better at some things than others. It's as if great college teachers are always exemplary, on all levels. You just rush them into any auditorium on a palanquin, press the start button, and they'll start dispensing wisdom around the class like an NBA point guard.

I sincerely doubt this is the case. Not all schools, classes, and learning contexts are the same. I don't know if a popular professor at MIT would necessarily be a hit at quirky, anarchic Marlboro College in Vermont, or vice versa (oh, check that! Marlboro College no longer exists). I am a capable undergraduate teacher, but I do a flimsy job with graduate students. Some professors have a special knack for working with Freshmen. Some don't. This is actually a really important thing for a school to know about its faculty. First-year students are at higher risk for everything from depression to dropping out.[19]

If we thought seriously about college teaching, we'd pay more attention to putting scholars in the "positions" where they excel. We'd assess who was good at what. We'd know who works well with at-risk students or kids with learning disabilities, and staff our departments accordingly. We are, I regret to say, a million, billion eons away from even starting a conversation of this nature. Oh, where oh where is the Dean of Pedagogy when we need her?

But the most insidious thing about Best Teacher talk is that it conveniently distracts us from what ails American Higher Education. Namely, that we have a lot of scholars who are poorly prepared and/or poorly paid to educate undergraduates. This is a *structural* problem. Graduate schools fail to provide the proper training in pedagogy. Administrations subject tenure-line faculty to student-negative Formulae. But most of all, these same administrations won't make the financial investments required to facilitate good teaching. A recent report echoes these sentiments charging that universities "do not seem to care about anything other than driving faculty costs to the lowest possible level."[20]

Seen in this light, Best Teacher chatter assumes a more sinister countenance. It asks us to gawk at those who somehow overcame immense, and *correctable*, structural obstacles. A Faculty of the Year award is a laurel that a college hands to itself. Christening Best Teachers is like a lily-white company congratulating itself on its diversity after hiring one African American Executive VP. It's like a catastrophe-inducing oil company releasing an ad about how it installed three temporary wind turbines in the name of sustainability.

***

Tributes to Best College Teachers do to professors what high fashion does to women—enslaves them to preposterous and unhealthy expectations of what constitutes The Beautiful in pedagogy.

I still don't have an answer as to why conversations around good teachers (and sometimes not so good ones) trigger exaggeration, exalted sentiments, and confetti. Educators, in any case, see that sort of hyperbole as inimical to the values of education. I could just as well do away with the entire, over the top, discourse. Less noise about "best" teachers might let us finally concentrate on the challenge of producing lots of good ones.

But let me be clear about something: on every campus in America, you *will* find good teachers. These are Liberal Arts professors, Contingent or tenure line, who are skilled, inspired, and committed educators. They perform all of the banal stuff mentioned above, because they realize that no student epiphany, no unexpected insight, no thoughtfulness, could occur without it.

These scholars may be in the minority, but they really do exist. They exist in spite of the absurdities of the tenure system. They exist in spite of the collapsed "job market." They exist in spite of thoughtless and frugal college administrations. They exist in spite of a Fuddy Duddy culture that worships Charmless Self-Absorption.

These people share one psycho-social characteristic in common: they exist in a tensile relation with their own profession. They do not share the priorities of their research-obsessed colleagues and managers. Good college teachers, then, don't necessarily do what is in their professional interest. They do what's in the interest of their students, Wall of Separation be damned. This is something *Mona Lisa Smile* intuited accurately.

8

FINDING YOUR GOOD COLLEGE TEACHER: THE ACTIVE LEARNING APPROACH

"The purpose of this course is to prepare you for your own death." These were the words allegedly proclaimed annually on the first day of class by some legendary Fuddy Duddy. It may be a completely apocryphal story, for all I know. But I recognize something in this statement that recommends its verisimilitude. I am speaking of the sheer gonzo madness, the utter outrageousness, the staggering indifference to sensitivities that I associate with a certain species of scholar.

I refer to these minor American icons as "Fun Professors." Along with those I call "Vaults of Erudition" and "Mentors," I consider them part of the 10 percent to 25 percent of college instructors, who perform well in the classroom. I won't call them the "Best College Teachers"—you now know how uncomfortable I am with that rubric. It would be more accurate to say that from a pedagogical perspective, they were the best thing professors had going in the second half of the twentieth century, when a stable tenure system still existed. They represented the standard of Teaching Excellence among the Liberal Arts faculty. Granted, this is a standard that was never particularly well thought out. Nor was this standard exceedingly high. Still, I think the contributions of these instructors ought be recognized.

I'd like to offer you an imaginative portrayal of these archetypal Scholar-Teachers. My portrait will not be uniformly flattering—hyperbole is the enemy of the Beautiful in pedagogy. But let there be no doubt, these Fun Professors, Vaults, and Mentors were *good* college teachers.

I do need to warn my reader, especially my reader selecting a school, that what has been traditionally considered "good" college teaching is now being radically rethought. Of late, Educational Scientists have advocated a very different approach to undergraduate instruction. It goes by the name of "Active Learning." We'll survey this method and assess the fairly dramatic threat to the status quo that it presents.

If it does catch on, then it will completely alter our conception of what needs to happen in a college classroom. Those who attend schools that subscribe to an Active Learning philosophy will receive a substantially *different* education. And, who knows, maybe it will help Humanists finally figure out what our "metric" for effective teaching might be.

The Fun Professor

Everyone remembers a Fun Professor or two from college (though probably no more than that). FPs have an uncanny ability to get, and subsequently hold, the attention of students. They are relentlessly *engaging*. Time moves swiftly in class. Students don't necessarily mind coming to the lectures. This may be correlated with the FP's penchant to make the material—no matter what it may be—interesting and relevant to their lives.

In an effort to captivate their audience, Fun Professors might devote the first five minutes to bantering with students about the parties they all attended last night. During their lectures, they'll drop F-bombs. They'll recount interesting and highly inappropriate personal anecdotes. They might even fling chalk and markers around the room. This reminds us of their genetic affinities to another type of professor: The Mentally Imbalanced Professor.

My Fun Professor was a philosopher, a short, middle-aged guy with a booming, nasally voice. He talked nonstop. But when he did pause to recognize our presence, the man had a penchant for raising existential dilemmas that induced tachycardia in our young breasts. During his discussion of John Stuart Mill's "On Liberty," he probed the relation between suicide and the state. "What if," he wondered aloud, "the police found out that a sophomore was not in our class today because he was entertaining suicidal thoughts?"

While students subtly glanced right and left for absentees who might fit the bill, he queried: "Could the authorities preemptively kick down the door to his dorm, and incarcerate him, in order to save his life?" "Hell no!" we riposted, nearly in unison. It was 1985. The youth was far less trusting of authority back then.

If there is one thing FPs hate, it's classroom consensus. So, the philosopher interrogated his auditors until he found the contrarian that suited his purpose. She reminded us that suicide is not all fun and games. Some municipal employee would have to scrape and hose that sophomore off the sidewalk (assuming a plunge from a dorm window—itself an act that endangered others). Suicide, she declaimed, was not merely a personal decision. The act had ramifications beyond the individual. Ergo, a state had a right to regulate, sanction, and ultimately forbid, this act.

"But what if," interjected another student to a smattering of lurid giggles, "you committed a suicide that burdened no one?" The example he gave—the kid clearly did not think this one through—went as follows: A man digs a six-foot hole. He then climbs inside his coffin. He has three friends lower the box into the ground. They shovel the dirt on top of the casket. The suicide calmly listens to the band Tears for Fears on his Sony Walkman as he asphyxiates. "How does any of that," he thundered, "inconvenience the state?" "Well then," declared the philosopher interrupting the macabre hush that this example had elicited, "the state would have to prosecute three accomplices to murder." We gasped as one. College!

Because of their tendency to provoke and enrage, Fun Professors are often thought to be "political." I am guessing some FPs were, privately, "on the Left." Yet, in the classroom their fealty was less to dogma than to a certain conception of unrestricted free speech that transcended political affiliation. Call it *academic* free speech—a way of discoursing that is more about the means than the end.

FPs are not trying to persuade you to adopt a specific political position. They *are* trying to move you from where you stand—wherever that may be—to some place that you're not standing and have never stood before. And will likely never stand again. The ability to induce this type of mental agility is what "critical thinking"—that tired old cliché—must entail. For a few hours a week, students get spun *away* from opinions they hold dear.

Critics of the Liberal Arts see this as an "academic" exercise—a pointless waste of time. Activists on the Left don't like it because it doesn't lend itself to social change. Religious traditionalists are deeply suspicious of "critical thinking" insofar as it is the solvent of dogma. Free Market fetishists would rather that class time be spent teaching students how to read a spreadsheet or repair a carburetor.

Which brings us to our most vocal detractors: conservatives complain about politicized college courses in which Leftist scholars indoctrinate America's youth. Those things happen, yes. But as we shall see in Chapter 9, what the Conservatives do not grasp is that: a) the 1960s are over, b) students dislike having their consciousness raised, and c) the fastest way to get 95 percent of your class to tune out is to browbeat them with that odd mix of incomprehensibility and I-detest-the-West sanctimony that is the hallmark of the contemporary American radical Left.

Fun Professors are fun, in part, because their ideology is complex, or odd, or inscrutable. They understand that in the Liberal Arts, we are training people *how* to think, not *what*, to think. This doesn't mean we are apolitical. We are definitely not. It does mean that a classroom is a space—one of the few remaining spaces—that invites rather rough treatment of my politics *and* yours, your aesthetic *and* mine. We must be eternally grateful to Fun Professors in particular for consecrating that space.

That space, I regret to say, is under threat. There is a tendency of those on the Right, especially since 9/11, to rail against professors who say things within class, or outside of class, that are perceived as seditious. Those on the Left are impatient with speech that is shocking, offensive or "triggering." In the academic context, this refers to the possibility that students may have a negative reaction to certain types of words, phrases, texts, images and ideas.[1]

Some college administrations and legal departments are asking professors to issue "trigger warnings." Thus, a professor is obliged to alert students to the presence of violent or graphic content in class materials. Where does that leave the intellectually trigger-happy Fun Professor? That discussion about suicide from 1985, with its playful allusions to dead teenagers, might well have raised hackles today. Anyone who sees this scenario as far-fetched does not understand the Cotton-Mather-Gleefully-Executing-Witches hysteria that can rapidly engulf a modern college campus. It's not a coincidence that the few Fun Professors who are still around today, tend to be Full Professors.

Vaults and Mentors

The Fun Professor maintains an unspoken campus rivalry with another iconic scholar: The Vault of Erudition. The Vault's superpower consists of the ability to transfix students while (and in spite of) transmitting staggering reserves of dense scholarly wisdom.

The first thing you notice about these women and men is that they are *learned*. (The second thing you notice is how oddly dressed they are.) The Vault's eloquence and quirkiness suggests to impressionable young minds that they are in the presence of an oracle. This is an impression that the Vault does not labor to dispel.

Let me immediately stress that *all* scholars are Vaults of Erudition. Every professor is insanely learned about his or her area of expertise—that is what ten years of graduate training will do. What distinguishes the Vaults from lesser Vaults (lockers?) is their capacity to enchant listeners. Most professors stagger and limp through their lectures. The Vaults, by contrast, are endowed with a flowing, spellbinding, lyrical style.

As with FPs, the Vaults are, ideologically speaking, hard to decipher. In fact, the Vault consistently negates the relevance and worth of the political sphere. Classic Vaults believe that nothing in the contemporary world is as important as what they are expounding upon in class, be it texts translated into Sanskrit from Chinese in the tenth century AD, or the Quebec Act of 1774. It is as if the present world only has value insofar as it permits us to live, breathe, reproduce and further acquaint ourselves with the Vault's area of expertise.

Back in 1990, I had the opportunity to closely observe a Vault in action. He was a distinguished scholar of ancient Near Eastern languages and literatures who believed that no contemporary dilemma was interesting or, in fact, relevant. My peek inside the Vault occurred during the lead up to the first war in Iraq. At that time, some campus rabble-rousers were expressing dismay that a return of the draft was imminent. To which the Vault's lectures seemed to whisper the subtext: "*Fear not, my children! Since at least the time of Hammurabi, this region has witnessed strife unceasing. If you are dragooned and, ultimately, are slain in Mesopotamia, you will fulfill a tragic, but ultimately, banal destiny. Are we not all foreordained to perish? Let us reflect, shall we, on that luminous passage from the Epic of Gilgamesh?*

'*Who, my friend can scale he[aven]?
Only the gods [live] forever under the sun.*

As for mankind, numbered are their days;
Whatever they achieve is but the wind!' [2]

Do not those words, my young colleagues, put your minds at ease?"
Unlike the FP, The Vault doesn't need to be charming or
funny in class, though on occasion she or he is droll. The FP
titillates and provokes listeners. The Vault awes them by sheer
breadth of knowledge. The FP crosses boundaries of good taste.
The Vault is prim; mastery of subject matter *is* the embodiment
of good taste. Classroom discussion with FPs is spirited but
sporadic. With Vaults it is nearly nonexistent. Vaults consider
the transmission of scholarly insight to be a sacred task. They'll
be damned if some junior is going to interrupt that diffusion
with a stupid question or aside.

This brings us to our third archetypal professor. These
would be the Mentors—scholars who cultivate lasting, professional relationships with their students. The mentor-mentee
association begins, often accidentally, when students come to
visit during office hours. Yet, over the semester and across the
years, their interactions intensify. What ensues is an ongoing,
unfolding acquaintance, usually about a student's professional
future. The Mentor is that person that a gowned student hugs
awkwardly while receiving her degree on stage at graduation
ceremonies.

I teach at a Jesuit university with a deep, historical commitment to mentorship. When I meet graduates, they often remi-
nisce about a priest on the faculty who greatly influenced their
lives. They fondly remember lengthy conversations with these
clerics about every conceivable topic—not just career decisions.
Alums speak of these encounters as the most meaningful, plea-
surable, and formative experiences they had in college.

I may be wrong, but at most other schools women faculty members are much more likely to play this role. The same holds true for African American professors, Latinos, Gay, and Lesbian scholars, and others in minority groups. They are often sought out by students, and not just students who share those identities.

Mentors, by the way, are almost never rewarded for performing this service. Few tenure and promotion Formulae that I have ever seen take stock of this work. These professors engage in mentorship simply out of good will, a sense of duty.

I draw no conclusions about what Mentors do *in* the classroom. In theory, they could be loathsome pedants. Statistically speaking, most probably are subpar teachers. The point is that the work they do, one-on-one, with students, is *invaluable*. Mentors pay attention to individuals outside of the classroom. The new approach that we are about to survey seeks to make that a reality inside the classroom.

Active Learning

When an FP or Vault lava-spews flaming chunks of wisdom for the duration of a lesson, this is referred to as "Passive Learning." In this format, "students passively receive information from the professor and internalize it through some form of memorization."[3]

When I was an undergraduate, with the exception of language classes, *all* learning was passive learning. The classroom was the locus of ceaseless, though sometimes quite remarkable, professorial monologues. These characters were like indomitable wind-up toys. They'd set their own clockwork motors running at 10:00 a.m. The gears and levers of their frenzied minds and maws would buzz, whirr, and clatter nonstop for seventy-five minutes. Some of us liked it. Most of us did not. But no one ever imagined it could be otherwise.

Well, nothing fires the imagination quite like looming fiscal and existential crises. So, when the Obama Administration proposed in 2013, unexpectedly, to link federal student aid to an "outcomes-based" ranking system for undergraduate institutions, colleges sort of took note of that.[4] When the Arizona State Legislature in 2015 slashed and gashed funding for public universities, folks paid attention.[5] When Wisconsin Governor Scott Walker proposed cutting $300 million to the University of Wisconsin system, even Fuddy Duddies emerged from their carrels.[6]

In recent years, imaginative alternatives to passive learning have surfaced. These are generally parsed under the rubric of something called "Active Learning." The concept likely came to the fore in the 1980s.[7] But it is only in the last quarter century or so—which coincides with an era in which politicians make menacing gestures toward Higher Ed—that the new method has been implemented with varying degrees of commitment.

The meaning of Active Learning is not entirely agreed upon. One researcher laments that the concept "has a history of vague definitions and nebulous descriptions."[8] Some view it as anything *but* "listening passively to an instructor's lecture."[9] For others, it connotes "any instructional method that…requires students to do meaningful learning activities and think about what they are doing."[10] "Learning is not a spectator sport," aver two of the major thinkers in this movement. "Students," they continue, "must talk about what they are learning, write about it, relate it to past experiences and apply it to their daily lives."[11]

Whatever one means by "Active Learning," there are count-less ways to put it into play. [12] Even fielding questions, which almost all instructors do, is a way of combatting passivity. Yet, the Active Learning model, as I understand it, is gunning for something much more substantive. It tries to involve students in the learning process not sporadically, but *consistently*. The professor's primary task, then, is to create an environment in which students are in a state of constant cognitive motion.

The most well-known term connected with Active Learn-ing is "the flipped classroom." Colloquially, this means students effectively lead the class and professors remain in the back-ground. This is somewhat imprecise. Specialists define flipped learning as "a set of pedagogical approaches that: 1) move most information-transmission teaching out of class, 2) use class time for learning activities that are active and social, and 3) require students to complete pre- and/or post-class activities to fully benefit from in-class work."[13]

As for the learning activities, scholars have suggested all sorts of options with that corny nomenclature one expects from Educational Scientists. The North Dakota State University Col-lege of Arts, Humanities, and Social Sciences website proposes Active Learning techniques like "Idea Wave," "Jigsaw Team-work," "Muddiest Point," and "Write/Pair/Share."[14] Still, other experts recommend "using debates, games, and role play."[15] And who can forget my personal favorite, "The Fishbowl"?[16]

All of these are undoubtedly fine suggestions—whatever the hell they might be. Let me recommend, however, one very basic rule of thumb for those who are new to this method: *the professor should speak less and listen more*. Herein lies a threat to the Fun Professor and Vault's way of life as we know it.

Speaking less means covering less material in class. Researchers call this dilemma the "coverage problem."[17] A colleague, schooled in the traditional approach, once mentioned to me that by semester's end she has shared only *one percent* of what she knows about her subject matter with her students. The newfangled method is going to cut that one percent figure by more than half. When I started my career as an apprentice Fun Professor, I would monologue during 95 percent of class. Now that I'm transitioning to an FP/Active Learning Hybrid, the number is 40 percent and dropping each semester.

When I first made the switch, I felt irresponsible. Lecturing less felt tantamount to ripping students off. Weren't they and/or their parents paying good money, I asked fuddyduddily, to listen to *every single thing* I knew about my subject matter? Dear reader, I now realize that I was wrong.

8 to 15

Active Learning environments in the Humanities are, ideally, small (i.e., fifteen to twenty in a class). Students thus have an interest in coming prepared, if only because they will be speaking for most of the class. If they come unprepared, they'll be embarrassed when I call on them. They'll get that frozen, scared bunny look, which I admit cracks me up. Their participation grades will plummet. They simply can't hide as their ancestors did under the half millennia reign of the passive regime.

When I teach a work of fiction, I am now in the habit of circulating a list of ten to twelve prompts in advance of class. Some questions might be straightforward (i.e., "who is our narrator, and how does he go about telling this story?"). Some might be more complex ("what specific meta-fictional elements do you notice in this novel?"). Some have no right answer ("when Marcia Umanoff says on page 360 'without transgression there isn't very much knowledge, is there?' Is this true within the storyworld of the text? Is this true in real life?").[18]

I would have covered all of these issues had I simply lectured. In a way, I want the students to deliver my lecture for me. If all goes well, they will do precisely that, and then some. It's the "and then some" that I find most intriguing. It's the "and then some" that flips the class from classical music (where we read according to a script) to Jazz (where unexpected things are likely to occur).

As the conversation begins, it becomes pretty clear to me who is reading and thinking intently about the material. And who is not. In the old days, I could only intuit who was righteous once I gave them a test or an essay weeks later. Now, the feedback loop is immediate and for slackers, brutal.

In every class I've ever taught, there has always been a minimum of three "ringers," students who seem genetically engineered to amaze me. Gosh, I love those kids! Yet, in a class of fifteen, that leaves twelve who don't initially amaze me. In other words, *it's not the students ranked 1 to 3 that I need to worry about, but 8 to 15* (4 to 7 are doing fine; I just wish they'd party less and read more carefully). When a classroom is flipped and students are all exposed and incapable of retreating into their shells, then I can really get to know (and ideally help) 8 to 15. I am not entirely sure how 8 to 15 feels about this. But who cares? I am convinced that they are going to learn more.

The method then forces professors to be mindful of *all* students. The closest analogue I can think of is college language instruction. I did this for about seven years, and I assure you this is exhausting work. The instructor has the responsibility of monitoring every student's every utterance. Moreover, active methods lead to unpredictable and often fascinating conversations. In my own area of expertise, there are insights that I only chanced upon because students drew it to my attention. It's almost like crowd sourcing interpretations of literature.

But does it work? As with many things in the field of educational research, there is no solid consensus. Still, many have concluded that the active method is superior.[19] One important study avers: "the combined data supports the hypothesis that the academic gains due to active learning...are *statistically significant*, and there is more consistency in the *overall performance* of active learners than for traditional learners."[20]

Some have countered, justifiably, that Active Learning is not a panacea.[21] My claim is *not* that professors experimenting with Active Learning methods are all exemplary Scholar-Teachers. A feckless instructor can sabotage whatever advantages the method might possess. Too, I have heard anecdotal reports of professors who game the system. Their cynical interpretation of Active Learning consists of imploring students to "discuss" for an hour or so, while they furtively read *The Jacobin* on their mobile devices.

My claim *is* that college shoppers and professors need to recognize what this method might do to Higher Education. If Active Learning becomes widely implemented, everything we know about undergraduate instruction is going to change. Even classrooms will change. They will have to be physically redesigned to accommodate small, face-to-face learning. This would be a radical departure from current lecture halls. It's quite fascinating, is it not, that these are modeled on educational spaces "that first appeared in medieval universities."[22]

Moreover, if massification is the plague, then Active Learning may be the antidote. At its best, the method virtually compels professors to pay attention to individuals.[23] The long-term trend in American Higher education is toward the depersonalization of the relation between students and professors. The new approach, by contrast, demands intellectual intimacy. For it to work, countless exchanges and interactions between teacher and pupil must take place in each session. If this method forces us to re-personalize our encounter with undergraduates, then that will be a felicitous development for all and sundry.

***

If there is a cinematic or literary depiction of a magnificent professor rocking some Active Learning techniques (like the Fish Bowl), then I am currently unaware of its existence. The method is likely too new for Hollywood to hype. Writers of fiction, who would instinctively pillory this method in a short story or novella, have yet to do so. Then again, Active Learning is probably a tricky thing to film or narrativize—what with all those empowered young minds speaking up. On whom would the camera focus? Say what you will about Passive Learning, but it's easier to represent in an artistic medium.

This being said, the new approach forces us to rethink those traits that we might usually associate with good college teaching. Both FPs and Vaults are endowed with the rare talent to set an eighteen- to twenty-four-year-old student's curiosity aflame. They achieve this through humor, outrageousness, dazzling rhetoric, or narrative virtuosity (but not political partisanship). These teachers draw people in—a true pedagogical gift. Few have it, and it's a very hard skill to learn. Though I do think we need to acknowledge what the limitations of this gift might be.

Good teachers, undeniably, engross students. But that's only part of the challenge. They must ascertain whether the engrossment is leading to actual learning. Experience has taught me that even students who are mesmerized by my lectures, who dig the cut of my jib, who nod their heads appreciatively at my every utterance (and even when I cough) might hand in piss-poor essays. A very underappreciated teacherly skill is understanding when your students don't understand. You see what I am saying?

Passive learning lacks an immediate feedback mechanism. It is thus difficult for teachers to monitor students. It's even more difficult if the instructor is so into himself/herself that she never takes students into consideration. The same self-indulgence that powers an uproarious classroom rant or a bravura lecture may be a lethal vice for an educator. Sometimes, the sheer force of the FP or Vault's personality, thought and rhetoric becomes the dominant feature of a semester's work. Students certainly savor the spectacle. Yet, what do they learn?

FPs and Vaults direct their brilliance to a collective known as a class. But *effective teaching always retains an individual dimension as well* (something that The Mentor intuits). Committed professors in the Humanities must focus on how a student writes, reads a text, reasons, speaks in public. Fun professoring and Vaulting, where so much depends on the sass, WOW! factor, and awesomeness of the instructor, can potentially relegate these skills to oblivion.

In short, good teachers think a lot about their students. In turn, their teaching engenders thoughtfulness. With that we arrive at my master metric for effective college instruction.

Like good art, good teaching colonizes your psyche. The novel ends, but you can't stop thinking about the characters. The film credits are rolling, yet you embark on a long meditation about a troubling scene. Class is over, but students are still pondering all that was said. Humanists, at their best, stimulate deep, unusual, unsettling, and omnidirectional thought in their charges. It is *thoughtfulness* that we are after. That's most likely to occur if we are as attuned to our students as they are to us.

9

SEX, SLOTH, SUBVERSION: THE PROFESSOR'S DAILY GRIND?

"[T]he daily life of a professor is not good narrative material."
—Elaine Showalter, *Faculty Towers:*
The Academic Novel and its Discontents

If most tenure-line professors do not spend much time teaching undergraduates, or thinking about undergraduates, or even setting foot on the campuses where dwell the undergraduates, then, *what precisely do most tenure-line professors do all day?*

Everyone seems to have an opinion—or fantasy—about this issue. For novelists, a professor, more often than not, cuts an erotic swath through the student body, and/or whatever other bodies might be around. For some conservative critics, professors sit around doing nothing.[1] For other conservative critics, shameless political indoctrination of student minds is how professors spend their semesters and trimesters.

Sex, sloth, subversion—provocative as each of these explanations may be, none really captures the word-and-thought-defying banality of a scholar's daily grind. Let's examine each (false) accusation in turn. This will help us understand what professors *actually* do all day and why that needs to change.

Hot Professor-On-Student Action?

Elaine Showalter's review of Tom Wolfe's 2004 campus novel *I Am Charlotte Simmons* is a most bloody piece of work. To borrow a line from Philip Roth, her critique made "Macduff's assault upon Macbeth look almost lackadaisical."[2]

The Princeton professor and former president of the Modern Language Association bristled at "Peeping Tom's Juvenile Jaunt."[3] The heroine of Wolfe's story, Charlotte Simmons, is a talented, thoughtful, beautiful, and virginal co-ed from backwoods Appalachia. The novel chronicles her disillusioning freshman year. Her school's combination of affluence, date-rape-y frat boys, academic excellence, and D1 basketball obsession led many to surmise that Duke University was being lampooned.

Writing in *The Chronicle of Higher Education*, Showalter spews invective at the mischievous white-suited writer. She describes Wolfe's tale as "bitchy, status-seeking, and dissecting."[4] The work is tarred as "puerile rubbish," for its "leering exposé of the sexual shenanigans of undergraduates."[5] What seems to most incense Showalter is the author's fixation on hooking up. "Titillated by the sexual revolution that has arrived on campus since his own student days," huffs Showalter, "Wolfe totally misses the feminist revolution that has given us so many more women students, faculty members, deans, and presidents."[6]

Even if we concur that the responsibility of a novelist is to celebrate the accomplishments of the feminist revolution, I still think Wolfe's intervention is intriguing. *I Am Charlotte Simmons* is pervaded by sexual tension and sexual violence. None of these interactions, however, occur between professors and students. The author's refusal to employ that shopworn plot device is significant in the following bipartite respect.

First, Wolfe's tale marks a conspicuous break with recent campus novels. In many of those stories, professor/student carnality—almost always involving an older man and a younger woman—figures prominently. The aforementioned Philip Roth, for example, canvassed this turf in *The Professor of Desire* (obliquely), *Sabbath's Theater*, and *The Dying Animal*. The male protagonist of his landmark 1974 *My Life as a Man* refers to female undergraduates as "forbidden daughters" and relays this startling pedagogical recollection:[7]

> *"But I love you! I want you!" I shouted at the slender girl who only the week before had bicycled in sneakers and a poplin skirt to English 312, her straw-colored hair in braids and her innards still awash with semen from our lunchtime assignation in her rented room.*[8]

Epic teacher/pupil fornication is a go-to in the campus novel genre. But the well-read Wolfe, who was surely familiar with the trope, does not go there. Why Showalter fails to notice this—*how* Showalter fails to notice this—is puzzling. In her own study, entitled *Faculty Towers: The Academic Novel and its Discontents* she argued that "sexual harassment" was "the dominant plot of the *Professorroman*" in the twenty-first century.[9] Well, Wolfe's yarn subverts her "randy professor" category.[10]

This leads us to the second way in which *I Am Charlotte Simmons* transcends the "voyeurism" which Showalter accuses it of purveying.[11] Wolfe has grasped something elemental about how professors and students interact nowadays. That is to say, they don't interact much at all. In the novel, as in real life, their encounters are incidental, instrumental, stilted, and uninspiring.

Given the absence of generalized professor-student contact, it is not coincidental that the era of professor-student romance has been drawing down for decades. We *should* thank the Feminist Revolution for that. Since the 1980s, a very stringent series of campus policies aimed at neutralizing predatory, "lecherous professors" have been enacted.[12] Largely effective, these regulations have rendered unwanted sexual attention by teachers toward undergraduates exceedingly rare. That's the good news. Now, for the bad news: the new policies gave non-predatory professors (i.e., most professors) license to cut themselves off from students. A license which they eagerly exploited.

Consensual professor-student romance is also extremely infrequent; neither students nor professors are really into it. Then again, there is always the occasional sophomore Free Spirit who concludes that what she must have in her life is a married forty-six-year-old professor with a Dad Bod, three kids, and a fondness for leather jackets. When students and professors who are both into it somehow stumble across one another, all sorts of complex moral dilemmas arise.

On many campuses, a professor will be dismissed should the HR department find out about his or her dalliance with an undergrad. According to this mandate, it matters not if the latter is, or ever was, in the former's class. I am reminded of a tale in which a scholar was brought up on these very charges. He did not deny the accusation. But he then stunned his interrogators with a clarification: at the time of that coital act most foul, he was unaware that the sophomore was a student in his class of 400. This is yet another reason to put an end to massification once and for all!

In any case, professor-student sex is more fiction than fact. Even professor-professor sex, outside the bonds of monogamous union, is pretty rare as well. Campuses may have been fleshpots back in 1975 when Malcolm Bradbury wrote *The History Man*. A modern Liberal Arts faculty, however, is more chaste than a theological seminary. Wolfe got it right: the carnal energy on campus radiates outward from the student dorms, not the English Department.

Sloth?

Sex with undergraduates is not really a scholar's cup of tea. Which is good. Nor is teaching undergraduates. Which is bad. As with everything about the contemporary professoriate, this insight needs to be understood in light of our obscene two-tiered system.

Non-tenured scholars (e.g., adjuncts, Visiting Professors, Professors of the Practice) devote considerable efforts to their teaching gigs. For about fifteen to twenty hours a week they'll be lecturing students. Let's not forget time spent preparing class, grading assignments and commuting. Their lack of job security also means that they are constantly tracking down jobs—their next jobs.

As for the tenure-line professors, they spend their days either: 1) not teaching, 2) scheming ingenious ways to not teach, or 3) complaining about their seven to ten hours of weekly teaching. Part reflex, part survival strategy, this behavior is corrosive on so many levels. When these scholars shun the lectern, they blow a freshman-dorm-sized hole into the available instructional faculty. By now, the reader knows what the consequences are: non-tenured professors are hired at low wages to fill in the vacuum.

To outsiders, understandably, this creates the impression that tenure-line professors are slugabeds and layabouts. They don't ever appear to be around. If and when they are present, they look sullen and distracted. Now, it is undeniable that one will find Associates and Fulls who conform to this stereotype (but never Assistants; those folks don't have the luxury of apathy). These Deadwoods are remarkably adept at sluffing off work or just disappearing. Then again, in the past few decades, administrations have become remarkably adept themselves at hounding these people into action or retirement.

For the most part, however, the tenured are *constantly, ceaselessly, relentlessly, working.* Any spouse of any academic— assuming he or she hasn't filed for divorce by now—can testify to the sheer bottomlessness of professorial toil. Granted, tenure-line professors spend little time with students. This should not obscure the fact that these scholars are always on duty. They rarely ease up.

This is because tenure-line professors are afflicted by a crippling dependency: all are peer-review junkies. All they want to do is publish more and more (and more) articles, chapters, and monographs. They want their work to be published by the handful of journals and presses that every other scholar is obsessed with as well. The competition is fierce (and occasionally rigged). This results in undergraduates being left cruelly unattended, like an addict's dog.

Outside of submitting research to peer-reviewed outlets, tenured scholars have other daily activities to pursue. These might be categorized under the rubric of "office politics." Even if professors never published a word, these endeavors would be enough to keep them busy from 9-5.

One type of scholar devotes herself to her department. She lives for her unit and plots a thousand-year growth plan. This type of office politics, on the face of it, seems like a harmless and even benevolent predilection. The downside is that in the collapsing, zero-sum world of the Humanities, building up your department often necessitates the complete annihilation of another. Fealty to one's department turns docile, harmless Fuddy Duddies into scowling, sideways-glancing hyenas.

Squabbles within departments are known to all professions. Any unit at any company can fall prey to factionalism and internecine strife. This is not unique to the Ivory Tower. Hostility *between* departments, however, is something different altogether. I know of no corporate parallel that approximates the spectacle of two academic units going to war with one another. Even if something similar does occur at a consulting firm or financial services company, could the hostilities possibly last for decades? Could the aggressions possibly continue in a manner that levels everything in the vicinity and reduces productivity to nil?

I still bear the psychic scars of a particularly vicious conflict waged between Romance Languages and the Comparative Literature departments a long time ago. That battle irrevocably altered about a dozen academic careers. A small platoon of Contingent faculty was road killed. About fifty other faculty members from other units were sucked into the combat and could not attend to their professional duties. There were many (threatened) lawsuits. One near physical altercation. I don't think the students much benefited from it either.

I actually can't recall what the fight was about. No matter: there was a principle involved. But I can't recall that either. Too, I remember a lot of *running*—late Friday afternoon sprints to the copying machine to reproduce and then deliver, before 5:00 p.m., the documents that would vindicate us in the eyes of the administration. This is odd because an Iron Law of Academe is that Fuddy Duddies never accelerate. Doubly odd, because a second Iron Law is that administrators rarely intervene in our idiotic conflicts. I guess that's probably another difference between Academe and every other functioning workplace in America.

Those fighting intra- and inter-departmental battles are pretty darn pathetic. I won't deny that. In our defense, however, we are invested in the future of our institution; we actually believe that if that new tenure-track line goes to us—and not to those morons over there—our school will be a better place. This is not the case, however, for professors whose allegiance is to their area of specialization, not their department or school. These scholars turn their backs almost entirely on their own colleagues. Their focus is directed toward networking with other specialists in their field, around the country, and around the world.

Thus, the expert in Joseph Conrad completely ignores his peers in the English Department. He cares not a wit about their coming campaign to recommend tenure for a beloved colleague, who regrettably has only published one book review in the past six years. Nor does he involve himself in the war-game exercises that are being conducted in anticipation of a row with the Spanish Department. He doesn't do office politics.

Rather, our Conradist wishes to correspond exclusively with other Conradists at other universities. This entails editing the flagship journal (*Joseph Conrad Studies*), sitting on various steering committees (The Mid-Atlantic Society for Joseph Conrad Studies), and quality controlling the types of papers that will be presented at this year's academic conference in Delaware (i.e., Con(Rad)ing: Carceral Discursivities, Extreme Violence, The Feminine Subject, and the Circulation of Capital in *The Secret Agent*).

The forgoing remarks remind us that, outside of publication, professors devote great energy to accumulating power. It might be soft power. As when a bunch of professors lobby on behalf of that iffy tenure candidate mentioned above. It might be stealth power. As when a chairperson furtively snags a couple of vacant offices for her department (and away from another). It might be a power trip. As when the Conradist exacts revenge upon a few renegade Conradists, the ones who had the *audacity* to not cite his article in their recent edited volume. Well guess who's paper submission for the "Con(Rad)ing" conference in Wilmington was rejected, bitches?

Subversion? (Politics and Network Power)

Ask conservative commentators what scholars do all day and they'll have an answer at the ready: professors ram Liberal dogma down the throats of unsuspecting youth. Colleges and universities, the Conservatives contend, have been flipped into mass indoctrination camps. The ruling Liberals, they allege, have purged all those who disagree with them from the faculty ranks. One Fox News personality even urged "affirmative action" to safeguard professors of more Rightward persuasions.[13]

This analysis is correct in certain respects and misleading in others. There is no doubt that there is a troubling dearth of Conservative scholars in Higher Ed.[14] One will find small clusters of them in Law Schools, B-Schools, and theological seminaries (where, depending on the denomination, they might be in the majority).[15] But their spotty presence in elite Liberal Arts colleges, and near invisibility in the Humanities, is unfortunate for all.

Just as multi-cultures are better than monocultures, having a variety of ideological viewpoints on campus makes everyone smarter. It also keeps people honest, militates against Group Think, etc. With these concerns in mind, a group of generally conservative academics, flying under the banner of the "The Heterodox Academy," has created a website that ranks colleges on their ability to accommodate divergent opinions. Their allegation is that "many academic fields and universities currently lack sufficient viewpoint diversity—particularly political diversity."[16]

I agree. Earlier, I talked about our twisted and corrupt hiring protocols for new faculty. Why do we have rigid orthodoxies in the humanities? Because professors do a woeful job of hiring people to the tenure track, and administrations can't or won't intervene. So, here's my unsolicited advice to deans and provosts alarmed about the inexplicable pro-Maoist drift of their English Department: it's about the search committees, stupid.

A second commonly heard conservative criticism, however, is less convincing. Most of these commentators assume that the principle fault line in Higher Ed lies between Conservatives and Liberals. They thus impose the Red State/Blue State division of American political culture onto American academic culture. This is mistaken; the more meaningful political fissure lies elsewhere.

For the past three decades, Liberal professors in the Humanities have been outthought, outpublished, outgeneraled, and outhired, by the Radical Left. There are thus not two, but *three* broad political columns in Academe: 1) a tiny cohort of conservatives, 2) a much larger, but graying and listless group of traditional Liberals, and 3) a burgeoning, *and much more institutionally influential and powerful* group of scholars on the extreme Left. In fact, they are so far to the Left that they sometimes slide off the edges of the game board and reemerge, Atari-style, on the other side, brandishing positions that are congenial to the Right.

Conservative Cultural Warriors can't (or won't) tell Liberals apart from the Radical Left. Even progressive Liberals, such as the comedian Bill Maher, make this mistake. Maher routinely complains about "Liberals" being cowardly on Free Speech. He made this point when students and others petitioned to disinvite him from delivering a commencement address at UC Berkeley because of his past comments on Islam.[17] My hunch is that those protesting Maher's appearance were not Liberals.

That Liberals are not the Radical Left, and vice versa, becomes clear when we consider the following differences. Liberals didn't rhapsodize over Iran's Islamist revolution in 1979, as did Michel Foucault, the patron saint of academic radicals.[18] Liberals don't believe that America ought suffer, in the words of a Columbia University professor, a "million more Mogadishus," after eighteen American soldiers were killed there in 1993.[19] Liberals don't maintain that the victims of 9/11 were "little Eichmanns"—a now infamous formulation composed by the then-University of Colorado Professor Ward Churchill (who has since been fired).[20] Liberals don't whip themselves up into a frenzy over the legitimacy of the State of Israel, a position associated with another icon of the Left, Edward Said, and his innumerable academic progeny.

Then, there are those Radical Left positions that have a weird way of sharing common ground with right-wing world-views. Liberals don't mistrust science, reducing it to a front for patriarchy, Eurocentrism, heterosexism, colonialist violence, and Western hegemony. Liberals don't view the Enlightenment as a centuries-long human rights catastrophe. Liberals don't draw moral equivalence between radical Islamist regimes and secular democracies. Strangely, these are issues where Leftists and certain Conservatives may converge.[21]

Liberals *will* accept that scholars who hold these positions deserve to be heard, assuming they are properly credentialed. Which raises another crucial difference between Liberals and Radicals—one that Bill Maher misunderstood during his UC Berkeley episode. Liberals do not share the Radical Left's willingness to curtail free speech. They are made uncomfortable by everything from Trigger Warnings, to the ritualistic shunning of campus speakers whose views some students find offensive.

Aside from confusing Liberals with Radicals, Conservative critics also err when they charge that these "Liberal" professors indoctrinate their students. This may have been a standard practice half a century ago, but the times they have 'a changed. The Wall of Separation between students and professors is real and substantial.[22] Little about the way students and professors interact nowadays makes it likely that the latter will propagandize the former.

Undergrads, for their part, simply don't have that sort of awe for their teachers anymore. They have the internet at their fingertips—where anything Professor says can be discredited. And they don't have the time to hang on to their teacher's every word, anyway. College students are severely cross-pressured by financial and time constraints. Only under exceptional circumstances will their busy schedules permit them to attend a "teach-in."

As for professors, few of them possess the charisma, or charm, or verbal sorcery, required to brainwash students. What is even more important is that very few scholars have the inclination to do so. This is because those with serious research profiles and World-Shattering Radical Ideas *no longer see the undergraduate classroom as the medium through which to disseminate their World-Shattering Radical Ideas.*

Scholars of the Radical Left—or any other political position—will most effectively promulgate their ideology by teaching *doctoral* students. If those students do get tenure-track jobs somewhere, then a political worldview becomes encrusted in a new institution for decades. Pepper the best graduate programs in the country with a dozen or so of your PhDs and, yes, in some very limited way, you are establishing a posterity for your World-Shattering Radical Ideas. The mission then is to colonize other faculties and build your empire.

Undergraduates, by contrast, are generally not worth the effort. They often come to class late, drunk or hungover, or all three. Half of them don't even do the reading. Unlike graduate students, they tend to mouth off when they disagree with you. Studies show that any attempt to raise their political consciousness can have precisely the opposite effect. In other words, they gravitate away from the professor's preferred ideology.[23]

The operative rule for an ideologue, then, goes like this: *you disseminate your politics by increasing your institutional power.*

This is far more effective than relying on undergraduate lectures as a vehicle for social change. In other words, effective ideological dissemination occurs when your network dominates a given field of inquiry. So much so, that there aren't many other perspectives around for anyone else to consider. The politicized professor likes the idea that you could walk from one side of campus to another and never find an alternative to his worldview. That's the stuff! And if you drive over to a school in any other state and still can't find an alternative there either, then it's all to the good.

The ability to control institutions (e.g., departments, learned societies, journal boards, committees, etc.) is the fever dream of *all* academic ideologues, on the Right or the Left. What must be stressed is that scholars of the Radical Left are, presently, really good at playing this game. For all of their theoretically dense and intellectually abstruse scholarship, these professors evince a single-mindedness in pursuing well-paid work for their colleagues that would make any union boss blush.

The Radical Left is many things. But its many microschools of thought also comprise one vast and highly successful tenure-and-promotion network. Its professors' relentless focus on placing their doctoral students in tenure-track jobs, logrolling via glowing letters of recommendation for promotion, green lighting each other's publication projects, is the stuff of legend in the academy. This is especially evident in fields like English, Comparative Literature, Women's Studies, Cinema Studies, Art History, and so forth.

What concerns me, then, is not the stray lecturer who invites students to political rallies. That simply annoys me. What concerns me (and should concern the college bound) is a department where nearly *every single* tenure-line professor in its employ reflexively attends the same rallies. What concerns me is the existence of entire subdisciplines where scholars who wouldn't attend these rallies happen to be the ones whose career prospects are diminished.

***

Tenure-line professors pass their days (and nights and weekends and summers) reading, researching, and writing. They also attend to the banal power plays that constitute the office politics of academic life. As they age, they increasingly spend their time reviewing the work of other professors. They might do that as reviewers for journals, or as outside evaluators for tenure and promotion cases. While scholars are busy doing all that stuff, they are simultaneously—effortlessly, in fact—doing one other thing: languishing in near total obscurity.

Think of it this way: Jill Lepore, Harold Bloom, Judith Butler, and Cornel West are among the most well-known Humanists in the country. The Harvard historian Lepore, because she writes for the *New Yorker* with its hefty readership of cultivated lay people. Bloom, because for decades he was an authoritative voice on what seemed to be the entire canon of Western literature. UC Berkeley's Butler (who critics see as a paragon of anti-Humanism), because of her status as an edgy philosopher of the Academic Left.[24] And still, with the exception of Cornel West—who is a pretty singular and mesmerizing figure—most Americans have never heard of them. What also must be stressed is that for every Lepore, and Bloom, and Butler that you might conceivably have heard of, there exist, let's say, a 100,000 humanists whom you've never heard of. And never will.

Don't feel bad, reader. The truth is that most scholars relish their obscurity. The only attention they crave is from the dozens of colleagues who also labor in their micro-field. To work on one's research project in the dungeon of the archive, away from the crowd, away from admins, away from undergraduates—*that* is what professors dream of doing all day. There exists a fine fit, then, between Humanists who do not seek a wider audience and a wider audience that does not seek them.

All of this helps explode another myth about professors. In the popular imagination, a scholar is often imagined to be an intellectual. According to the stereotype, an "intellectual" is a cosmopolitan, a sophisticate, the fount of bold, riveting, ingenious, and contrarian thoughts. An intellectual is also a person who *seeks* an audience, looks for trouble. Yet, today's shy and retiring professor is, more often than not, a provincial. A Footnote Yokel. A Brand Ambassador for Fussiness. A high-functioning shut-in, and not really the person you wish to be seated next to at a dinner party. If you're looking for an intellectual, then hang out with a novelist, not some misted-over micro-specialist.

Higher Education is going to change. Higher Education *is changing already*. Not coincidentally, a rather salient prescription of this book might be phrased as: "*Professor, you must change as well!*" Later, I'll propose that we radically rethink the graduate school experience. All the better to reduce the number of future peer-review junkies. All the better to train creative, spry thinkers who can improvise as their predecessors' way of life comes to an end.

As for present generations strung out on the tenure line, their path to rehabilitation is less clear. I frankly do not know how we go about treating their addiction to obscurity, obscurantism, and incommunicability. All I can do is rearticulate one core truth about us and hope for the best. Scholars possess a work ethic unmatched by nearly any other professionals. The challenge for thoughtful administrators consists of incentivizing them to direct those impressive energies elsewhere, outward, ideally toward undergraduates. If professors awake eager to teach, listen, and interact with their students, it might portend a New Day for us.

CONCLUSION

THE END: CULTIVATE YOUR GARDEN

*"Cela est bien dit, répondit Candide, mais
il faut cultiver notre jardin."*
—Voltaire, *Candide, ou l'optimisme.*

America's system of Higher Education is currently misaligned, uncoordinated, out of sync with itself. What it just can't figure out is how to link the professional and intellectual interests of scholars with the needs of undergraduates—like their need to be properly educated. It's a crippling asymmetry, decades in the making, demoralizing to contemplate, and with no simple solution in sight.

This disconnect is especially pronounced at elite institutions. Which is why I urge all to be wary of colleges and universities that soar high and lofty atop the *U.S. News & World Report* rankings. Throughout this book, I argued that there is no correlation between Dream Schools and teaching excellence.

In fact, the dreamier the school the less likely its most valued professors will be engaging with undergraduates. The less likely it promotes a culture that emphasizes educating eighteen-to twenty-four-year-olds. The less likely its distinguished faculty view teaching as the life's calling that it surely is.

I'd be the first to admit that there are many phenomenal things about an elite school. There's the preposterously accomplished student body. These people—the carefully curated collection of young folks with splendid talents and abilities with whom you will fraternize—might be the single most compelling draw to such a place.[1] There's the library—oh the exquisite stacks! There are the many well-published scholars whose massive tally of Google Scholar Citations demonstrates the esteem in which others hold their research. But when it comes to professors as teachers (and strangely, as we saw in Chapter 6, sometimes even as researchers), the less storied campuses actually may have more to offer.

Excellent instruction and pedagogical innovation are much more likely to occur at so-called second-tier and lower first-tier schools. Among those are Honors Colleges, SLACS, HBCUs, and religious institutions. I recommend that prospective students research these schools alongside the obvious Destination Colleges. I advise my reader to view them not merely as "safetys" but as contenders.

There are dozens of these hidden gems, unknown seats of learning where students come first. I hope that another contrarian professor lights them up for the college-bound to inspect. That's the book about higher education we really need. Some author(s) will chart the bestsellers' list by producing *A Guide to Great Colleges as Professors Lay Dying*. The writer will offer sage advice to Generation Alpha and what's left of Gen Z. Using metrics, a dash of AI and a ton of human insight, this guide-book will identify America's most pedagogy-positive schools.

The present contrarian professor simply reminds applicants that hype and oversell are the lingua franca of the college admissions process. This leaves the consumer in a vulnerable position. Prior to investing a quarter-million dollars in tuition, you will need to make educated guesses. Your challenge consists of looking for clues that a school is genuinely realigning the work of its faculty with the intellectual needs of its students.

As for student needs, those have been catalogued through-out this book. Taking a preponderance of courses capped at fifteen or so undergraduates is important. Studying with faculty who are well treated by the institution and incentivized to work with you is important. Having the opportunity to be mentored by professors is important. Knowing an institution's pedagog-ical philosophy is important (assuming it actually has one). As you bear all that in mind, ignore the "Best Teacher" hype and focus on quality instruction *across* the faculty. Attending a school with a genuine culture of learning in which professors are deeply invested not only in the success of their own classes but also of the entire curriculum is most important of all.

All these deliverables are to be supplied by professors, and here is where the aforementioned disconnect sets in. The profes-sors aren't trained to supply these goods, nor are they interested in providing them. Administrators could of course financially incentivize professors to recommit to teaching, but they don't appear eager to make that investment either. Tenure's diminish-ment adds to all of these challenges. The fewer tenured scholars there are on campus, the more Contingent professors there will be. The latter, as we learned in this book, aren't expected to perform (or be compensated for) "Service"—and the build-out of a major or a curriculum is a service requirement. So, in a casualized labor force, which professors will create, implement and administer this new culture of learning?

Colleges with genuine cultures of teaching and pedagogy are hard to create. Though the ones that can actually pull this off will eventually corner a massive, lucrative and evergreen market. That's the incentive: decades of robust student enrollments in exchange for a coherent vision and wise and humane treatment of scholars. Which institutions are willing to play "the long game" and invest accordingly?

The Interregnum

The First Golden Age of the American Professoriate, which stretched roughly from the era of the GI Bill after World War II to the turn of the millennia, is over. Who knows, maybe there will be a Second Golden Age later this century. Presently, however, we scholars inhabit a miserable interregnum. Our vocation is a dead man walking, a zombie, or some other metaphor that indicates we're faring forward, even though we are not entirely alive.

In the conclusion to the first edition of this book, I was guardedly optimistic that the professoriate could mount a comeback, snap itself back to life. Now, after the whiplash of two Trump administrations, the COVID plague (which I argued at the time only would accelerate the casualization of academic labor), and ceaseless unrest on college campuses, I have abandoned optimism.[2]

So, how's it going to go down, so to speak, for the American professoriate? The Red State public university systems will continue to de-tenure and DOGE their professors. These initiatives will synergize with the steady decades-long, pre-Trumpian decrease in tenure lines. Factor in that the average age of a tenured professor in the United States is roughly fifty-nine years old; a wave of retirements is on the horizon.[3] All of these variables should summate to lower the percentage of tenured professors (last measured at 23 percent) beneath the 20 percent mark by the 2030s.

At that point, we will have entered the Death Watch phase of the professoriate's downward spiral. I forecast a good degree of internecine strife. The levels of income and status inequality between scholars on any given campus will reach new highs (and moral lows). The rapidly shrinking, about-to-bottom-out, tenured minority will possess job security, reasonable guaranteed salaries, and academic freedom protections. The rapidly expanding non-tenured majority will enjoy none of those perks. How could any of this possibly go wrong?

Cunning admins will devise ways to set the unequal ranks of professors against one another. Even in the best of times, Fuddy Duddies were never known for their "guild solidarity." Wily administrators across the country will figure out how to divide and conquer (one emerging strategy consists of appointing Contingent faculty to positions of leadership, like dean or chair, in which they govern tenured faculty). These de-solidarizing tactics will immunize administrations from general strikes, faculty-wide protests, "Hey Hey! Ho Ho!" chants and whatnot.

Maybe the corporate suits will push it too far, as corporate suits are wont to do. Maybe their avarice and short sightedness will spark the collective rage that will inaugurate the Second Golden Age. Until then, the coming decades in Academe will feature a good deal of infighting and finger pointing.

Let's recall, however, that the tenure system is still sputtering along, still on autopilot, still coughing up what I referred to as "lottery winners." It's a hard number to gauge, but by my reckoning some 25,000 to 50,000 people in the United States were granted tenure in 2024. This fresh young cohort of zombies, presently in their late thirties and early forties will play out the string of their careers for decades to come. I predict that in the 2070s, there will be a journalistic genre of stories about "The Last Tenured Titan" or "The Final Fuddy Duddy." The long-form articles will feature some cane-wielding and cane-thrusting savant prattling on about Foucault. Their tales will be narratively compelling—a cross between the pathos of the character played by Pamela Anderson in *The Last Showgirl* and the melancholy of *The Moor's Last Sigh*.

If I am ever consulted as to what professors must do to stave off this scenario, I'd try to frame my answer in terms of the need for a reset, a tearing down, a complete rethink of everything we do as scholars. The challenge, I'd affirm, lies in finding ways to seamlessly integrate teaching *and* research. That organic unity has been cleaved by an ethos of scholarly micro-specialization. This ethos devalues skills like the ability to communicate with large audiences. In doing so, it de-democratizes the transmission of knowledge. Knowledge, in this understanding, is aimed squarely at the types of people you spent time with in grad school.

My alternative would implore scholars to think of their research's "end user" *not* as another scholar, but as an undergraduate and more broadly a cultivated lay person. Our reset would force us to completely reframe how we think of scholarly research. Its new goal would be to de-complexify. It would demand we pursue research questions with the expectation that we must be able to explain our findings to students and compa-triots. Take something incomprehensible and make it as com-prehensible as possible! Clarify or perish! That's the new ethos.

Such an interactive orientation would likely alter the very nature of scholarly production in the humanities. We'd strive to create knowledge that stimulates non-scholars to think about the things that we as scholars think about. It doesn't mean the finished research would be less scholarly, less born of intense study, less based on erudite reflection. It just means we want the research to target a different audience.

The scholar who studies, let's say, Voltaire would not aim to produce specialized work about the philosopher's thought that only a few colleagues could comprehend. Instead, this person would gear their research to broader publics. What did Voltaire—that scandalous curmudgeon whose books were impounded and whose battles with the powerful were legend-ary—want us to reflect upon? And regardless of what this very odd savant wanted, what does his thought force us to contem-plate about religion, global affairs, violence, the abuse of power, and extreme human folly?

In the meantime, until this interregnum passes, the only clear moral action available to professors is this: day in and day out, we should aspire to teach well. Ideas are like seeds, classrooms are like gardens. Good preparation, crafting clear lesson plans, avoiding ideological rigidity—these are essential professorial habits that will sprout in our students' minds. As the world is falling down around us, that's all we can do. We can cultivate our gardens. Now, we must all go and work in our gardens.

ENDNOTES

Preface to the Second Edition: As Professors Lay Dying

[1] Jacques Berlinerblau, "They've Been Scheming to Cut Tenure for Years. It's Happening," *The Chronicle of Higher Education*, February 1, 2023, https://www.chronicle.com/article/theyve-been-scheming-to-cut-tenure-for-years-its-happening. Please recall that initiatives such as "de-tenurification" or "post-tenure review" (see below) will also pressure tenured professors to curtail their expressive liberties.

[2] Emily J. Levine, "Academic Freedom's Origin Story," *Stanford Report*, March 1, 2023, https://news.stanford.edu/stories/2023/05/origin-story-academic-freedom.

[3] Stanford Eugenics History Project, "Edward Ross," accessed March 30, 2025, https://www.stanfordeugenics.com/edward-ross.

[4] Katherine Knott, "Trump Taps J.D. Vance, Sharp Critic of Higher Ed, for VP," *Inside Higher Ed*, July 16, 2024, https://www.insidehighered.com/news/government/politics-elections/2024/07/16/trump-taps-jd-vance-sharp-critic-higher-ed-vp.

[5] John Curtis, "Table 3: Trends in Faculty Employment Status, 1975 and 1976 to 2011," in *The Employment Status of Instructional Staff Members in Higher Education, Fall 2011* (American Association of University Professors, 2014), 5, https://www.aaup.org/sites/default/files/files/AAUP-InstrStaff2011-April2014.pdf.

[6] Ibid.

7   Ibid.

8   Glenn Colby, *Data Snapshot: Contingent Faculty in
    US Higher Ed* (American Association of University
    Professors, March 2023), 2, https://www.aaup.org/sites/
    default/files/AAUP%20Data%20Snapshot.pdf.

9   Ibid.

10 Barrett J. Taylor and Kimberly Watts, "Tenure Bans: An Exploratory
    Study of State Legislation Proposing to Eliminate Faculty Tenure,
    2012–2022," *The Review of Higher Education*, published ahead of
    print (March 2023), 9, https://muse.jhu.edu/article/934009/pdf.

11 Ryan Quinn, "The Growing Trend of Attacks on Tenure," *Inside
    Higher Ed*, August 5, 2024, https://www.insidehighered.com/news/
    faculty-issues/tenure/2024/08/05/growing-trend-attacks-tenure.

12 Marc Stein, "The End of Faculty Tenure and the Transformation of
    Higher Education," *Academe*, Winter 2023, https://www.aaup.org/
    article/end-faculty-tenure-and-transformation-higher-education.

13 Paul Weinstein Jr., "Administrative Bloat at U.S. Colleges Is
    Skyrocketing," *Forbes*, August 28, 2023, https://www.forbes.com/
    sites/paulweinstein/2023/08/28/administrative-bloat-at-us-
    colleges-is-skyrocketing/.

14 Jon Marcus, "Bureaucratic Costs at Some Colleges Are Twice What's
    Spent on Instruction," *American Council of Trustees and Alumni*,
    July 25, 2017, https://www.goacta.org/news-item/bureaucratic-
    costs-at-some-colleges-are-twice-whats-spent-on-instruction/.

15 Lee Gardner, "The Campus Cold War: Faculty vs.
    Administrators," *The Chronicle of Higher Education*, March
    7, 2025, https://www.chronicle.com/article/the-campus-
    cold-war-faculty-vs-administrators. According to a 2022
    Chronicle analysis cited in the article, at least 141 faculty
    bodies voted no confidence in their leaders between 2012 and
    2021—nearly triple the 50 recorded in the prior decade.

16 National Center for Education Statistics, "Table 315.10. Number
    of Faculty in Degree-Granting Postsecondary Institutions, by
    Employment Status, Sex, Control, and Level of Institution:
    Selected Years, Fall 1970 Through Fall 2022," *Digest of
    Education Statistics 2023*, accessed March 31, 2025, https://
    nces.ed.gov/programs/digest/d23/tables/dt23_315.10.asp.

17 Josh Gruenbaum, Sean R. Keveney, and Thomas E. Wheeler,
    letter to Dr. Katrina Armstrong and David Greenwald,

March 13, 2025, https://static01.nyt.com/newsgraphics/
documenttools/6d3c124d8e20212d/85dec154-full.pdf.

[18] Rashid Khalidi, "Does Columbia Still Merit the Name of
a University?" *The Guardian*, March 25, 2025, https://
www.theguardian.com/commentisfree/2025/mar/25/
does-columbia-merit-the-name-of-university.

[19] Charlie Eaton, "15 Billion is Enough to Fight a
President," *The New York Times*, March 25, 2025,
https://www.nytimes.com/2025/03/25/opinion/
trump-university-endowment-spending.html.

[20] Evan Goldstein and Len Gutkin, "'It Is Remarkable How
Quickly the Chill Has Descended,'" *The Chronicle of Higher
Education*, March 25, 2025, https://www.chronicle.com/article/
it-is-remarkable-how-quickly-the-chill-has-descended.

[21] Chris Rufo, *America's Cultural Revolution: How the Radical
Left Conquered Everything* (Broadside Books, 2023), 3-42.

[22] Jacques Berlinerblau, "When Your Next College Free Speech
Controversy Erupts, Don't Blame Liberals," *The Washington
Post*, June 30, 2017, https://www.washingtonpost.com/news/
grade-point/wp/2017/06/30/when-your-next-college-free-speech-
controversy-erupts-dont-blame-liberals/; The correspondences
between far right and far left are discussed in Jacques Berlinerblau,
"Cheat Sheet for Political Secularism and Secular Studies," *Secular
Studies* 5, no. 1 (2023): 53–56, https://brill.com/view/journals/
secu/5/1/article-p53_10.xml?
language=en&srsltid=AfmBOoooIGVC9FrI98pnymRWPIjxPZO3
HYGxC2cnqxjSkQ7x33IRIqPG ; Jacques Berlinerblau,
Secularism: The Basics (London: Routledge, 2021),163–187;
Jacques Berlinerblau, "The Crisis in Secular Studies," *The
Chronicle of Higher Education*, September 8, 2014, https://
www.chronicle.com/article/the-crisis-in-secular-studies/.

Introduction

[1] John Curtis, "Table 3: Trends in Faculty Employment Status, 1975
and 1976 to 2011," in *The Employment Status of Instructional Staff
Members in Higher Education, Fall 2011* (American Association
of University Professors, 2014), 5, https://www.aaup.org/sites/
default/files/files/AAUP-InstrStaff2011-April2014.pdf.

2   Emily Yoffe, "Please Take the Gold Watch. Please!: The
    Abolition of Mandatory Retirement, and How It Changed
    America in Unexpected Ways," *Slate*, April 14, 2011,
    http://www.slate.com/articles/life/silver_lining/2011/04/
    please_take_the_gold_watch_please.html; Glenn Colby, "Data
    Snapshot: Tenure and Contingency in US Higher Education,"
    American Association of University Professors, March 2023,
    https://www.aaup.org/sites/default/files/AAUP%20Data%20
    Snapshot.pdf. About 24 percent of faculty members in US
    colleges and universities held full-time tenured appointments
    in fall 2021, compared with about 39 percent in fall 1987.

3   Glenn Colby, "Data Snapshot: Tenure and
    Contingency in US Higher Education."

4   Gary Saul Morson and Morton Schapiro, "Bullish on 2040,"
    The Chronicle of Higher Education, May 16, 2015, http://www.
    chronicle.com/article/2040-Prognosis-for-Higher/230295/.

5   Steven Shulman, *Faculty and Graduate Student Employment at
    U.S. Colleges and Universities, 2013*, Center for the Study of
    Academic Labor (Colorado State University, 2015): 1, https://
    csal.colostate.edu/docs/Employment-Report-2013.pdf ; John
    Curtis, "Table 3: Trends in Faculty Employment Status, 1975 and
    1976 to 2011," in *The Employment Status of Instructional Staff
    Members in Higher Education, Fall 2011* (American Association
    of University Professors, 2014), 5, https://www.aaup.org/sites/
    default/files/files/AAUP-InstrStaff2011-April2014.pdf.

6   "Table 105.20: Enrollment in Elementary, Secondary, and
    Degree-Granting Postsecondary Institutions, by Level and
    Control of Institution, Enrollment Level, and Attendance
    Status and Sex of Student: Selected Years, Fall 1990 Through
    Fall 2025," in *National Center for Education Statistics*, accessed
    November 15, 2016, http://nces.ed.gov/programs/digest/
    d15/tables/dt15_105.20.asp?current=yes. According to Best
    Colleges, "U.S. College Enrollment: Trends and Statistics,"
    updated March 5, 2025, https://www.bestcolleges.com/research/
    college-enrollment-statistics/, 19 million students are enrolled
    in U.S. colleges — 16 million in undergraduate programs.

7   U.S. News & World Report, "Annual Tuition and Fees
    for Full-Time Students at Leading Universities in the
    United States in 2024/25," *Statista*, accessed March

20, 2025, https://www.statista.com/statistics/200867/ annual-tuition-and-fees-at-leading-universities-in-the-us/.

[8] Richard Arum and Josipa Roksa, *Academically Adrift: Limited Learning on College Campuses* (University of Chicago Press, 2011), 121.

[9] Mitchell E. Daniels, Jr., "An Open Letter to the People of Purdue," Purdue University, January 18, 2013, accessed July 1, 2015, https://www.purdue.edu/newsroom/archive/ releases/2013/Q1/an-open-letter-to-the-people-of-purdue.html.

[10] "The Teaching of the Arts and Humanities at Harvard College: Mapping the Future," Harvard University, May 31, 2013, https://scholar.harvard.edu/files/ jamessimpson/files/mapping_the_future.pdf.

[11] Andrew Hacker and Claudia Dreifus, *Higher Education? How Colleges Are Wasting Our Money And Failing Our Kids — And What We Can Do About It* (Henry Holt and Company, 2010), 77.

[12] "Fast Facts," National Center for Education Statistics, accessed November 15, 2016, https://nces.ed.gov/fastfacts/display. asp?id=37. According to Wade Zhou, "STEM is the New Liberal Arts: The Changing Trends of College Majors," *The Kansas City Star*, July 29, 2024, https://www.kansascity.com/news/business/ article290538154.html, between 2013 and 2022, bachelor's degrees awarded by American colleges increased from about 1.85 million annually to just over 2 million. During this period, the number of STEM bachelor's degrees rose by about 40 percent, while the number of bachelor's degrees in liberal arts and humanities awarded per year fell by 14 percent during the same time period.

[13] Wade Zhou, "STEM is the New Liberal Arts: The Changing Trends of College Majors."

Chapter 1: Fuddy Duddies

[1] Tom Wolfe, *The Bonfire of the Vanities* (Farrar, Straus, Giroux, 1987), 360.

[2] Zadie Smith, *On Beauty* (Penguin Books, 2005), 15.

[3] Nathaniel Hawthorne, *Fanshawe*, in *Nathaniel Hawthorne: Collected Novels: Fanshawe, The Scarlet Letter, The House of the Seven Gables, The Blithedale Romance, The Marble Faun* (Library of America, 1983), 76.

4   Kingsley Amis, *Lucky Jim* (New York Review of Books, 1953), 2.

5   David Lodge, *Changing Places: A Tale of Two Campuses,
    in The Campus Trilogy* (Penguin Books, 1975), 35.

6   J.M. Coetzee, *Disgrace* (Penguin Books, 1999), 3.

7   Anne Bernays, *Professor Romeo* (Penguin, 1989), 94.

8   In 2004, the median time to complete a PhD in the humanities
    was 9.7 years. See Terry Evans, et al., "Global Forms and Local
    Forces: PhD Enrollments and Graduations in Australia, Canada,
    the Czech Republic, the United Kingdom, and the United States,"
    in *Globalization and Its Impacts on the Quality of PhD Education*,
    ed. Maresi Nared and Barbara Evans (Sense Publishers, 2014), 75.

9   Chris Golde, "The Role of the Department and Discipline in
    Doctoral Student Attrition: Lessons from Four Departments,"
    The Journal of Higher Education 76, no. 6 (2005): 669;
    Frim Ampaw and Audrey Jager, "Completing the Three
    Stages of Doctoral Education: An Event History Analysis,"
    Researching Higher Education 53 (2012): 640–660.

10 The Graduate Assembly, "Graduate Student Happiness &
    Well-Being Report | 2014," *Berkeley University*, https://
    cshe.berkeley.edu/sites/default/files/wellbeing-slides-
    seru%2520%25281%2529%2520%25281%2529.pdf ;
    Jenny Hyun et al., "Graduate Student Mental Health: Needs
    Assessment and Utilization of Counseling Services," *Journal of
    College Student Development* 47, no. 3 (2006): 248, 255; Jenny
    Hyun, et al., "Mental Health Need, Awareness, and Use of
    Counseling Services Among International Graduate Students,"
    Journal of American College Health 56, no. 2 (2007): 110.

11 Galen Panger, Janell Tryon, and Andrew Smith, *Graduate
    Student Happiness & Well-Being Report* (Berkeley: Graduate
    Assembly, University of California, Berkeley, April 2015).

12 Richard Arum and Josipa Roksa, *Academically
    Adrift: Limited Learning on College Campuses*
    (University of Chicago Press, 2011), 133.

13 Doctoral candidates, observed Louis Menand almost fifteen
    years ago, are "being trained as specialists…for a scholarly
    and pedagogical world that is rapidly ceasing to exist." Louis
    Menand, "The Marketplace of Ideas," *American Council of
    Learned Societies Occasional Paper*, no. 49 (2001): 20.

Chapter 2: Who Is Your Professor 1?
"The Non-Contingent"

1   For a list of the many designations for Contingent faculty, see John Cross and Edie Goldenberg, *Off Track Profs: Nontenured Teachers in Higher Education* (MIT Press, 2009), 20.

2   Walter Metzger, "The 1940 Statement of Principles on Academic Freedom and Tenure," *Law and Contemporary Problems* 53, no. 3 (1990).

3   Roger Geiger, *The History of American Higher Education: Learning and Culture from the Founding to World War II* (Princeton University Press, 2015), 1.

4   American Association of University Professors and the Association of American Colleges, "1940 Statement of Principles on Academic Freedom and Tenure," accessed June 18, 2015, http://www.aaup.org/report/1940-statement-principles-academic-freedom-and-tenure.

5   Ibid.

6   Richard Hofstadter and Walter Metzger, *The Development of Academic Freedom in the United States* (Columbia University Press, 1955).

7   Fascinatingly, it also sought to tilt the balance of power to college and university presidents: for decades, they had sought a hedge against meddlesome trustees, governing boards, and other powerful outsiders. Walter P. Metzger, "The 1940 Statement of Principles on Academic Freedom and Tenure," *Law and Contemporary Problems* 53, no. 3 (Summer 1990): 74, https://scholarship.law.duke.edu/lcp/vol53/iss3/3.

8   American Association of University Professors and the Association of American Colleges, "1940 Statement of Principles on Academic Freedom and Tenure," accessed June 18, 2015, http://www.aaup.org/report/1940-statement-principles-academic-freedom-and-tenure.

9   The question of the irrevocability of tenure is taken up by William Van Alstyne in a famous 1971 article for the AAUP. The author there insists that tenure "lays no claim whatever to a guarantee of lifetime employment." He emphasizes that tenure *does* guarantee due process for those whose tenure is subject to being revoked. The argument strikes me as theoretically true but empirically

false. For all intents and purposes, tenured professors are hired for life, except in extreme and unusual cases. William Van Alstyne's "The Meaning of Tenure" is found in Matthew Finkin, *The Case for Tenure* (Cornell University Press, 1996), 3–9.

10 American Association of University Professors and the Association of American Colleges, "1940 Statement of Principles on Academic Freedom and Tenure," accessed June 18, 2015, http://www.aaup.org/report/1940-statement-principles-academic-freedom-and-tenure.

11 Walter P. Metzger, "The 1940 Statement of Principles on Academic Freedom and Tenure," *Law and Contemporary Problems* 53, no. 3 (Summer 1990): 8 and 12, https://scholarship.law.duke.edu/lcp/vol53/iss3/3.

12 Caitlin Rosenthal, "Fundamental Freedom or Fringe Benefit? Rice University and the Administrative History of Tenure, 1935-1963," *AAUP Journal of Academic Freedom* 2 (2011), 16; Walter P. Metzger, "The 1940 Statement of Principles on Academic Freedom and Tenure," *Law and Contemporary Problems* 53, no. 3 (Summer 1990): 4, https://scholarship.law.duke.edu/lcp/vol53/iss3/3.

13 An economist looking at job placement rates for recent PhDs in English notes that "of those who get tenure-track jobs, most get jobs at universities ranked lower than they attended." David Colander, "Where do PhDs in English Get Jobs?: An Economist's View of the English PhD Market," *Pedagogy* 15 (2015), 140.

14 Andrew Hacker and Claudia Dreifus, *Higher Education? How Colleges Are Wasting Our Money and Failing Our Kids — And What We Can Do About It* (Henry Holt, 2010), 13–14.

15 Andrew Hacker and Claudia Dreifus, *Higher Education? How Colleges Are Wasting Our Money and Failing Our Kids — And What We Can Do About It* (Henry Holt, 2010), 14.

16 Interestingly, Golden Boy was not hired. This development reminds me that in the financially strangled CUNY system, both professors and administrators understand that their mission is educating the working- and middle-class students of New York.

17 John Cross and Edie Goldenberg, *Off Track Profs: Nontenured Teachers in Higher Education* (MIT Press, 2009), 48.

18 Scott Jaschik, "Unhappy Associate Professors," *Inside Higher Ed*, June 3, 2012, https://www.insidehighered.com/news/2012/06/04/associate-professors-less-satisfied-those-other-ranks-survey-finds;

Jaschik is citing the result of the COACHE survey
conducted through the 2011 to 2012 academic year.

[19] Julie Striver, "The Immobility of the Associate Professor,"
Chronicle of Higher Education, September 19, 2006,
http://chronicle.com/article/The-Immobility-of-
the/46881; Striver, by the way, is a pseudonym.

[20] Quoted in Scott Jaschik, "Unhappy Associate
Professors," *Inside Higher Ed*, June 3, 2012, https://
www.insidehighered.com/news/2012/06/04/
associate-professors-less-satisfied-those-other-ranks-survey-finds.

[21] Robin Wilson, "Why Are Associate Professors So Unhappy?"
Chronicle of Higher Education, June 3, 2012, http://chronicle.
com/article/Why-Are-Associate-Professors/132071/;
Robin Wilson, "Associate Professors: Academe's Sandwich
Generation," *Chronicle of Higher Education*, July 24, 2011,
http://chronicle.com/article/Associate-Professors-/128302/.

[22] Julie Striver, "The Immobility of the Associate Professor,"
Chronicle of Higher Education, September 19, 2006, http://
chronicle.com/article/The-Immobility-of-the/46881.

[23] Robin Wilson, "Why Are Associate Professors So Unhappy?"
Chronicle of Higher Education, June 3, 2012, http://chronicle.
com/article/Why-Are-Associate-Professors/132071/.

[24] Neal Dow, "Terminal Associate Professors, Past and Present,"
Chronicle of Higher Education, March 26, 2014, http://chronicle.
com/article/Terminal-Associate-Professors/145537/; Scott
Jaschik, "Unhappy Associate Professors," *Inside Higher Ed*, June
3, 2012, https://www.insidehighered.com/news/2012/06/04/
associate-professors-less-satisfied-those-other-ranks-survey-finds.

[25] Peter Schmidt, "Talk of 'De-Tenure' Triggers Faculty Ire in
Tennessee," *Chronicle of Higher Education*, March 3, 2015, http://
chronicle.com/article/Talk-of-De-Tenure-Triggers/228097.

[26] Andy Thomason, "Wisconsin Regents Approve Post-Tenure
Policies Condemned by Faculty," *Chronicle of Higher Education*,
December 8, 2016, http://www.chronicle.com/blogs/ticker/
wisconsin-regents-approve-post-tenure-policies-condemned-by-
faculty/116042; Neal Dow, "Terminal Associate Professors, Past and
Present," *Chronicle of Higher Education*, March 26, 2014, http://
chronicle.com/article/Terminal-Associate-Professors/145537/;
Scott Jaschik, "Unhappy Associate Professors," *Inside Higher Ed*,

June 3, 2012, https://www.insidehighered.com/news/2012/06/04/associate-professors-less-satisfied-those-other-ranks-survey-finds.

Chapter 3: Who Is Your Professor 2? The Contingent

1. Arthur Wilke, ed., *The Hidden Professoriate: Credentialism, Professionalism, and the Tenure Crisis* (Greenwood Press, 1979).
2. John Curtis, "Table 3: Trends in Faculty Employment Status," *The Employment Status of Instructional Staff Members in Higher Education, Fall 2011* (American Association of University Professors, 2014), 5.
3. Ibid. This calculation is based on John Curtis's number of 1,059,179 Contingent Faculty in 2011.
4. John Cross and Edie Goldenberg, *Off-Track Profs: Nontenured Teachers in Higher Education* (The MIT Press, 2009), 9.
5. Steven Shulman, *Faculty and Graduate Student Employment at U.S. Colleges and Universities, 2013*, Center for the Study of Academic Labor (Colorado State University, 2015), accessed September 20, 2015, https://csal.colostate.edu/docs/Employment-Report-2013.pdf.
6. Stanford University, "Faculty Profile," *Stanford Facts*, Fall 2024, https://facts.stanford.edu/academics/faculty-profile/.
7. Steven Shulman, *Faculty and Graduate Student Employment at U.S. Colleges and Universities, 2013*, Center for the Study of Academic Labor (Colorado State University, 2015), accessed September 20, 2015, https://csal.colostate.edu/docs/Employment-Report-2013.pdf.
8. Ibid.
9. Ibid.
10. John Cross and Edie Goldenberg, *Off Track Profs: Nontenured Teachers in Higher Education* (MIT Press, 2009), 20–21.
11. Coalition on the Academic Workforce, "A Portrait of Part-Time Faculty Members: A Summary of Findings on Part-Time Faculty Respondents to the Coalition on the Academic Workforce Survey of Contingent Faculty Members and Instructors," (2012), 10, http://www.academicworkforce.org/CAW_portrait_2012.pdf; A different study found that the median annual teaching salary was $22,041. And, no, that does not include health insurance. House Committee on Education and the Workforce

Democratic Staff, "The Just-in-Time Professor: A Staff Report
Summarizing eForum Responses on the Working Conditions
of Contingent Faculty in Higher Education" (January 24,
2014), 6, http://democrats-edworkforce.house.gov/imo/
media/doc/documents/1.24.14-AdjunctEforumReport.pdf.

[12] Ibid., 6. One draws this conclusion on the basis of the
table entitled "Respondents' Annual Salaries."

[13] Ken Jacobs, Ian Perry, and Jenifer MacGillvary, "The High
Public Cost of Low Wages: Poverty-Level Wages Cost U.S.
Taxpayers $152.8 Billion Each Year in Public Support for
Working Families," *UC Berkeley Center for Labor Research and
Education* (April 2015), 3, http://laborcenter.berkeley.edu/
pdf/2015/the-high-public-cost-of-low-wages.pdf. See the table
entitled "Low-Wage Occupations and Public Assistance Rates."

[14] Steven Shulman, *Contingent Faculty Report* (Center for the
Study of Academic Labor, Colorado State University, 2015),
9, https://csal.colostate.edu/docs/Employment-Report-2013.
pdf Another study reports 50.8 percent of Contingent
instructional staff are women, see John Curtis, "Table 3: Trends
in Faculty Employment Status," in *The Employment Status
of Instructional Staff Members in Higher Education, Fall 2011*
(American Association of University Professors, 2014), 18.

[15] Matt Saccaro, "Professors on Food Stamps: The Shocking
True Story of Academia in 2014," *Salon*, September 21, 2014,
http://www.salon.com/2014/09/21/professors_on_food_
stamps_the_shocking_true_story_of_academia_in_2014/;
Laryssa Wirstiuk, "How eBay Subsidized My Academic
Career," *Chronicle of Higher Education*, June 22, 2015, http://
chronicle.com/article/How-eBay-Subsidized-My/230967/.

[16] Daniel Kovalik, "Death of an Adjunct," *Pittsburgh Post-
Gazette*, September 18, 2013, http://www.post-gazette.com/
Op-Ed/2013/09/18/Death-of-an-adjunct/stories/201309180224;
L.V. Andreson, "Death of a Professor," *Slate*, November 17,
2013, http://www.slate.com/articles/news_and_politics/
education/2013/11/death_of_duquesne_adjunct_margaret_
mary_vojtko_what_really_happened_to_her.html.

[17] Hamilton Nolan, "'Academic Apartheid in Higher Education,"
Gawker, June 8, 2016, https://www.gawkerarchives.com/
academic-apartheid-in-higher-education-1781357648.

18 John Curtis and Saranna Thornton, "Here's the News: The Annual
    Report on the Economic Status of the Profession, 2012-13,"
    Academe (March–April 2013): 7, fig. 1, "Trends in Instructional
    Staff Employment Status, 1975–2011, All Institutions, National
    Totals." Somewhat different tabulations appear in American
    Association of University Professors, *The Academic Workforce
    Data Tool*, accessed March 21, 2025, https://www.aaup.org/sites/
    default/files/files/AAUP_Report_InstrStaff-75-11_apr2013.pdf.

19 John Curtis and Saranna Thornton, "Here's the News." Somewhat
    different data points have been generated by a more recent study.
    See IPEDS Academic Workforce, "IPEDS Academic Workforce,
    Fall 2002 to 2023," *AAUP Data*, 2023, https://data.aaup.org/
    academic-workforce/, The study suggests that the category of
    non-tenure-track full time is unique in that it is growing across
    time. I discussed this data in Jacques Berlinerblau, "They've Been
    Scheming to Cut Tenure for Years. It's Happening" *Chronicle of
    Higher Education.* February 1, 2023, https://www.chronicle.com/
    article/theyve-been-scheming-to-cut-tenure-for-years-its-happening.

20 American Association of University Professors, "The Status of
    Non-Tenure-Track Faculty," *AAUP*, June 1993, http://www.aaup.
    org/report/status-non-tenure-track-faculty; A few years later,
    sustained attention to the topic was undertaken in Roger Baldwin
    and Jay Chronister, *Teaching Without Tenure: Policies and Practices
    for a New Era* (Johns Hopkins University Press, 2001), 77–113.

21 Roger Baldwin and Jay Chronister, *Teaching Without
    Tenure: Policies and Practices for a New Era* (Johns
    Hopkins University Press, 2001), 43.

22 David N. Figlio, Morton Schapiro, and Kevin Soter, "Are Tenure
    Track Professors Better Teachers?" *National Bureau of Economic
    Research*, Working Paper No. 19406, JEL No. I23 (September
    2013), 15; For a discussion of this study, see Dan Berrett, "Adjuncts
    Are Better Teachers Than Tenured Professors, Study Finds,"
    The Chronicle of Higher Education, September 9, 2013, http://
    chronicle.com/article/Ad-juncts-Are-Bet-ter/141523/; Eric B.
    Bettinger and Bridget Terry Long, "Does Cheaper Mean Better?
    The Impact of Using Adjunct Instructors on Student Outcomes,"
    The Review of Economics and Statistics 92, no. 3 (August 2010).

23   Audrey Jaeger and M. Kevin Eagan, "Examining Retention
      and Contingent Faculty Use in a State System of Public Higher
      Education," *Educational Policy* 25, no. 3 (2011): 531.

24   Paul Umbach, "How Effective Are They? Exploring the Impact
      of Contingent Faculty on Undergraduate Education," *The Review
      of Higher Education* 30, no. 2 (2007): 110; Cheryl Halcrow and
      Myrna Olson, "Adjunct Faculty: Valued Resource or Cheap
      Labor?" *Focus on Colleges, Universities, and Schools* 2, no. 1 (2008):
      5; Timothy Schibik and Charles Harrington, "Caveat Emptor:
      Is There a Correlation Between Part-Time Faculty Utilization
      and Student Learning Outcomes and Retention," *Association
      for Institutional Research* 91 (Spring 2004); Ernst Benjamin,
      "How Over-Reliance on Contingent Appointments Diminishes
      Faculty Involvement in Student Learning," *Peer Review* 5 (2002),
      https://www.nccft.org/wp-content/uploads/2020/01/How-Over-
      Reliance-on-Contingent-Appointments-Diminishes-Faculty-
      Involvement-in-Student-Learning-Association-of-American-
      Colleges-Universities.pdf; Daniel Jacoby, "Effects of Part-Time
      Faculty Employment on Community College Graduation Rates,"
      The Journal of Higher Education 77, no. 6 (2006): 1100.

25   Roger Baldwin and Matthew Wawrzynski, "Contingent
      Faculty as Teachers: What We Know; What We Need to
      Know," *American Behavioral Scientist* 55, no. 11 (2011):
      1505; Peter Schmidt, "Conditions Imposed on Part-Time
      Adjuncts Threaten Quality of Teaching, Researchers Say," *The
      Chronicle of Higher Education*, November 30, 2010, http://
      chronicle.com/article/Conditions-Imposed-on/125573/.

26   Jean Waltman, Inger Bergom, Carol Hollenshead, Jeanne
      Miller, and Louise August, "Factors Contributing to Job
      Satisfaction and Dissatisfaction Among Non-Tenure-Track
      Faculty," *The Journal of Higher Education* 83, no. 3 (2012).

27   Joseph Conrad, *The Secret Agent* (Penguin, 1907), 245.

Chapter 4: The Campus Tour: Teaching Excellence

1   Ronald Berk, *Thirteen Strategies to Measure
      College Teaching* (Stylus, 2006), 19–22.

2   Anne Boring, Kellie Ottoboni, and Philip B. Stark, "Student
      Evaluations of Teaching (Mostly) Do Not Measure Teaching

Effectiveness," *ScienceOpen Research* (2006); Lillian MacNell, Adam Driscoll, and Andrea N. Hunt, "What's in a Name: Exposing Gender Bias in Student Ratings of Teaching," *Innovative Higher Education* 40, no. 4 (2015); The findings seem to be consistent across time, see Susan Basow, "Student Evaluations of College Professors: When Gender Matters," *Journal of Educational Psychology* 87, no. 4 (1995); Also see Suzanne Young, Leslie Rush, and Dale Shaw, "Evaluating Gender Bias in Ratings of University Instructors' Teaching Effectiveness," *International Journal for the Scholarship of Teaching and Learning* 3 no. 2 (2009); As for race, see Gabriel Smith and Kristin J. Anderson, "Students' Ratings of Professors: The Teaching Style of Contingency for Latino/a Professors," *Journal of Latinos and Education* 4, no. 2 (2005); Of interest here is Therese Huston, compiler, "Research Report: Race and Gender Bias in Student Evaluations of Teaching," *Seattle University, Center for Excellence in Teaching & Learning* (2005) https://groups.google.com/g/usaafricadialogue/c/-DTQFVrWQWE ; Therese A. Huston, "Race and Gender Bias in Higher Education: Could Faculty Course Evaluations Impede Further Progress Toward Parity?" *Seattle Journal for Social Justice* 4, no. 2 (2006): art. 34, https://digitalcommons.law.seattleu.edu/sjsj/vol4/iss2/34.

[3] Meredith Adams and Paul Umbach, "Nonresponse and Online Student Evaluations of Teaching: Understanding the Influence of Salience, Fatigue, and Academic Environments," *Research in Higher Education* 53 (2012).

[4] Daniel S. Hamermesh and Amy Parker, "Beauty in the Classroom: Instructors' Pulchritude and Putative Pedagogical Productivity," *Economics of Education Review* 24, no. 4 (2005); Nalini Ambady and Robert Rosenthal, "Half a Minute: Predicting Teacher Evaluations from Thin Slices of Nonverbal Behavior and Physical Attractiveness," *Journal of Personality and Social Psychology* 64, no. 3 (1993).

[5] Peter Hoefer, Jack Yurkiewicz, and John C. Byrne, "The Association between Students' Evaluation of Teaching and Grades," *Decision Sciences Journal of Innovative Education* 10, no. 3 (2012); Anthony Greenwald and Gerald M. Gillmore, "No Pain, No Gain? The Importance of Measuring Course Workload in Student Ratings of Instruction," *Journal of Educational Psychology* 89, no. 4 (1997).

6   Philip B. Stark and Richard Freishtat, "An Evaluation of
     Course Evaluations," *ScienceOpen* (2014): 12; Bert Brockx,
     Pieter Spooren, and Dimitri Mortelmans, "Taking the Grading
     Leniency Story to the Edge. The Influence of Student, Teacher,
     and Course Characteristics on Student Evaluations of Teaching
     in Higher Education," *Educ Asse Eval Acc* 23 (2011).

7   Ben Schmidt, "Gendered Language in Teacher Reviews,"
     Benschmidt.org (2015), http://benschmidt.org/profGender;
     Claire Cain Miller, "Is the Professor Bossy or Brilliant? Much
     Depends on Gender," *The New York Times*, February 6, 2015,
     http://www.nytimes.com/2015/02/07/upshot/is-the-professor-
     bossy-or-brilliant-much-depends-on-gender.html?_r=0.

8   Ronald Berk, *Thirteen Strategies to Measure College Teaching*
     (Stylus, 2006), 19–22; Ronald Berk, "Survey of 12 Strategies
     to Measure Teaching Effectiveness," *International Journal of
     Teaching and Learning in Higher Education* 17, no. 1 (2005).

9   Richard Arum and Josipa Roksa, *Academically
     Adrift: Limited Learning on College Campuses* (The
     University of Chicago Press, 2011), 21–26, 145.

10   Ibid., 124.

11   Bill Gates, "National Governors Association Winter
     Meeting," speech, NGA, JW Marriott, Washington,
     DC, 2011, https://www.nga.org/wp-content/
     uploads/2021/04/2011NGAWinterMeeting.pdf; "Career
     Counselor: Bill Gates or Steve Jobs?" *The New York Times*, 21
     March 2011, http://www.nytimes.com/roomfordebate/2011/03/20/
     career-counselor-bill-gates-or-steve-jobs?src=tw.

12   Barack Obama, "Remarks by the President on College
     Affordability—Buffalo, NY," *The White House:
     Office of the Press Secretary*, August 22, 2013, https://
     www.whitehouse.gov/the-press-office/2013/08/22/
     remarks-president-college-affordability-buffalo-ny.

13   Valerie Strauss, "What GOP Platform Says on Education,"
     Washington Post, August 28, 2012, https://www.washingtonpost.
     com/blogs/answer-sheet/post/what-gop-platform-says-
     on-education/2012/08/28/4b993bce-f15a-11e1-892d-
     bc92fee603a7_blog.html; Eric Kelderman, "Where Scott Walker
     Got His Utilitarian View of Higher Education—and Why
     it Matters," *The Chronicle of Higher Education*, September 2,

2015, http://chronicle.com/article/Where-Scott-Walker-Got-His/232803/?cid=at&utm_source=at&utm_medium=en; Andy Thomason, "As Degrees Are Cut, Critics Continue to Decry Dismantling of U. of North Carolina," *The Chronicle of Higher Education*, May 27, 2015, http://chronicle.com/blogs/ticker/as-degrees-are-cut-critics-continue-to-decry-dismantling-of-u-of-north-carolina/99587; For a riposte to this species of thinking, see Eric Johnson, "Business Can Pay To Train its Own Workforce," *The Chronicle of Higher Education*, June 22, 2015, http://chronicle.com/article/Business-Can-Pay-to-Train-Its/231015/.

[14] David Hornsby and Ruksana Osman, "Massification in Higher Education: Large Classes and Student Learning," *Higher Education* 67 (2014): 712.

[15] Ibid., 713.

[16] For pre-calculus, see Rima Brusi, Arturo Portnoy, and Nilsa Toro, "Student Engagement and Completion in Precalculus, Precalculus Mega Section: Efficiently Assisting Student Engagement and Completion with Communications and Information Technology," *Journal of STEM Education* 14, no. 1 (2013); For macroeconomics, see Henry Raimondo, Louis Esposito, and Irving Gershenberg, "Introductory Class Size and Student Performance in Intermediate Theory Courses," *The Journal of Economic Education* 21, no. 4 (1990); For writing programs, see Alice Horning, "The Definitive Article on Class Size," *Writing Program Administration* 31, no. 1 (2007): 19–22.

[17] Iryna Johnson, "Class Size and Student Performance at a Public Research University: A Cross-Classified Model," *Research in Higher Education* 51 (2010): 701–723, 721; Michael Dillon, E.C. Kokkelenberg, and Sean M. Christy, "The Effects of Class Size on Student Achievement in Higher Education: Applying an Earnings Function," CHERI Working Paper #28 (2002): 14–15, http://digitalcommons.ilr.cornell.edu/cgi/viewcontent.cgi?article=1015&context=cheri.

[18] Jack Keil and Peter Partell, "The Effect of Class Size on Student Performance and Retention at Binghamton University," *Binghamton University: Office of Budget & Institutional Research* (1998), http://www.classsizematters.org/wp-content/uploads/2012/11/Class_size_jkpp1997.pdf.

19 Lauren Chapman and Larry Ludlow, "Can Downsizing College Class Sizes Augment Student Outcomes? An Investigation of the Effects of Class Size on Student Learning," *The Journal of General Education* 59, no. 2 (2010).

20 Michael Dillon, E.C. Kokkelenberg, and Sean M. Christy, "The Effects of Class Size on Student Achievement in Higher Education: Applying an Earnings Function," CHERI Working Paper #28 (2002): 5, http://digitalcommons.ilr.cornell.edu/cgi/viewcontent.cgi?article=1015&context=cheri; One recent study of *online* courses argues that class size may be irrelevant to student performance. These findings were discussed in Scott Jaschik, "Study Finds No Impact of Increasing Class Size on Student Outcomes," *Inside Higher Ed*, January 5, 2015, https://www.insidehighered.com/news/2015/01/05/study-finds-no-impact-increasing-class-size-student-outcomes; Another study of a pre-calculus module concluded that there exist ways of making larger classes better serve the needs of undergraduates. Rima Brusi, Arturo Portnoy, and Nilsa Toro, "Student Engagement and Completion in Precalculus, Precalculus Mega Section: Efficiently Assisting Student Engagement and Completion with Communications and Information Technology," *Journal of STEM Education* 14, no. 1 (2013): 20–25.

21 Joe Cuseo, "The Empirical Case Against *Large Class Size*: Adverse Effects on the Teaching, Learning, and Retention of First-Year Students," *The Journal of Faculty Development* 1, no. 17 (2007); Iryna Johnson, "Class Size and Student Performance at a Public Research University: A Cross-Classified Model," *Research in Higher Education* 51 (2010): 721; Felix Maringe and Nevensha Sing, "Teaching Large Classes in an Increasingly Internationalising Higher Education Environment: Pedagogical, Quality and Equity Issues," *Higher Education* 67 (2014); Edward Kokkelenberg, Michael Dillon, and Sean Christy, "The Effects of Class Size on Student Grades at a Public University" (Cornell Higher Education Research Institute, School of Industrial and Labor Relations, Cornell University, 2006), 13; Stephanie Allais, "A Critical Perspective on Large Class Teaching: The Political Economy of Massification and the Sociology of Knowledge," *Higher Education* 67 (2014); James Cooper and Pamela Robinson, "The Argument for Making Large Classes Seem Small," *New Directions for Teaching and Learning* 81 (2000): 13.

22   Henry Raimondo, Louis Esposito, and Irving Gershenberg, "Introductory Class Size and Student Performance in Intermediate Theory Courses," *The Journal of Economic Education* 21, no. 4 (1990): 379.

23   Lauren Chapman and Larry Ludlow, "Can Downsizing College Class Sizes Augment Student Outcomes? An Investigation of the Effects of Class Size on Student Learning," *The Journal of General Education* 59, no. 2 (2010): 118.

24   James Cooper and Pamela Robinson, "The Argument for Making Large Classes Seem Small," *New Directions for Teaching and Learning* 81 (2000): 13.

25   David Hornsby and Ruksana Osman, "Massification in Higher Education: Large Classes and Student Learning," *Higher Education* 67 (2014): 713.

26   Ibid.

27   Alice Horning, "The Definitive Article on Class Size," *Writing Program Administration* 31, no. 1 (2007): 19–22.

28   Corbin Campbell, "College Educational Quality (CEQ) Project," Teachers College, Columbia University, 2013 Pilot Study 1, *Technical Report* (2013): 3; The results are discussed in Dan Berrett, "A New Kind of Study Seeks to Quantify Educational Quality," *The Chronicle of Higher Education*, February 7, 2014, http://chronicle.com/article/A-New-Kind-of-Study-Seeks-to/144621/; For a caution about establishing any given number as equaling a "large class," see Felix Maringe and Nevensha Sing, "Teaching Large Classes in an Increasingly Internationalising Higher Education Environment: Pedagogical, Quality and Equity Issues," *Higher Education* 67 (2014): 763.

29   Corbin Campbell, "College Educational Quality (CEQ) Project," Teachers College, Columbia University, 2013 Pilot Study 1, *Technical Report* (2013): 3.

30   Dan Berrett, "U. of Georgia Bets $4.4 Million That Small Classes Can Bolster Learning," *The Chronicle of Higher Education*, September 8, 2015, http://chronicle.com/article/U-of-Georgia-Bets-44/232889/.

31   David Hornsby and Ruksana Osman, "Massification in Higher Education: Large Classes and Student Learning," *Higher Education* 67 (2014): 713.

32 James Lang, "Support Your Local Teaching Center," *The Chronicle of Higher Education*, July 20, 2007, http://chronicle.com/article/Support-Your-Local-Teaching/46606/.

33 "Other Teaching Centers—All U.S. Colleges and Universities," *The University of Kansas Center for Teaching Excellence*, accessed June 12, 2016, https://www.academia.edu/44899582/ANALYZING_FACULTY_LEARNING_STYLES_AND_LEARNING_CHOICES_IN_AN_ONLINE_ENVIRONMENT_FOR_FACULTY_PROFESSIONAL_DEVELOPMENT?uc-g-sw=19227666.

34 Derek Bok Center for Teaching and Learning, "About," accessed October 30, 2015, http://bokcenter.harvard.edu/about; Yale Center for Teaching and Learning, "Programs," accessed October 30, 2015, http://teaching.yale.edu/programs.

35 Angela Sorby, "Teaching and Learning About Teaching and Learning," *The Chronicle of Higher Education*, May 5, 2014, http://chronicle.com/article/TeachingLearning-About/146403/; Mary Deane Sorcinelli, "Ten Principles of Good Practice in Creating and Sustaining Teaching and Learning Centers," in *A Guide to Faculty Development: Practical Advice, Examples, and Resources*, ed. Kay J. Gillespie and Douglas L. Robertson (Anker Publishing Company, Inc., 2002), 9–23,https://www.researchgate.net/profile/Mary_Sorcinelli/publication/265655118_Ten_Principles_of_Good_Practice_in_Creating_and_Sustaining_Teaching_and_learning_Centers/links/54d2b7450cf28e06972668f7.pdf?__cf_chl_tk=GetHm9LUeKHUxrurVKEsmnLgsKwgf_HCpa5i1yxPzzk-1747161358-1.0.1.1-1MgjtMj1m_mo.wNEnxeWmDH5x6W9mlyrHZ0YOuUOYBU.

Chapter 5: Applying to the Right Colleges: A Cheat Sheet for Parents

1 Benjamin Ginsberg, "Table 4. Changes in the Supply of and Demand for Administrative Services, 1985-2005," in *The Fall of the Faculty: The Rise of the All-Administrative University and Why It Matters* (Oxford University Press, 2011), 28.

2 Scott Carlson, "Administrator Hiring Drove 28 percent Boom in Higher-Ed Work Force, Report Says," *Chronicle*

of Higher Education, February 5, 2014, http://chronicle.
com/article/Administrator-Hiring-Drove-28-/144519/.

3 Jon Marcus, "Death By a Thousand Emails: How
Administrative Bloat is Kill," *The Eye, The New England
Center for Investigative Reporting*, February 6, 2014, https://
www.goacta.org/news-item/bureaucratic-costs-at-some-
colleges-are-twice-whats-spent-on-instruction/.

4 Larry Gerber, *The Rise and Decline of Faculty Governance:
Professionalization and the Modern American University*
(Johns Hopkins University Press, 2014).

5 Michael Bérubé and Jennifer Ruth, *The Humanities,
Higher Education, & Academic Freedom: Three Necessary
Arguments* (Palgrave Macmillan, 2015), 89.

6 Steven Shulman, *Faculty and Graduate Student Employment at
U.S. Colleges and Universities, 2013*, Center for the Study of
Academic Labor (Colorado State University, 2015), https://
csal.colostate.edu/docs/Employment-Report-2013.pdf.

7 Joe Cuseo, "The Empirical Case Against *Large Class
Size*: Adverse Effects on the Teaching, Learning, and
Retention of First-Year Students," *The Journal of
Faculty Development* 21, no. 1 (January 2007).

8 Peter Schmidt, "University Honors Colleges Pitch the 'Liberal-Arts
College Experience,'" *Chronicle of Higher Education*, February
28, 2010, http://chronicle.com/article/University-Honors-
Colleges/64394/; The National Collegiate Honors Council has
900 affiliated members. "Join," *The National Collegiate Honors
Council*, accessed July 11, 2016, http://nchchonors.org/join/.

9 "Most Innovative Schools," *US News & World Report*,
accessed November 2, 2016, https://www.usnews.
com/best-colleges/rankings/national-universities/
innovative?_sort=rank&_sortDirection=asc.

10 Alan Hughes, "Tenure at Small Colleges," *Inside Higher
Ed*, August 10, 2014, https://www.insidehighered.com/
advice/2014/08/11/essay-earning-tenure-small-liberal-arts-colleges.

11 SLACs have passionate defenders. One thinks of Loren Pope's
*Colleges that Change Lives: 40 Schools That Will Change the
Way You Think About Colleges, 2nd Edition* (Penguin Books,
2006). Judging by its popularity, Pope's book tapped into
widespread dissatisfaction with Destination Colleges. As you

read this fierce reprimand to academic elitism, you encounter countless testimonials like this one: "Just a year at [College of] Wooster has changed my life, and I love my teachers. None of my friends who go to Penn or Brown talk about their teachers or what their school has done for them." Loren Pope, *Colleges That Change Lives* (New York: Penguin Books, 1996), 5.

12   "Academic Life," Smith College, accessed August 15, 2015, https://www.smith.edu/your-campus/offices-services/office-student-affairs/student-handbook/academic-life.

13   "Meredith College," Women's College Coalition, accessed August 15, 2015. http://womenscolleges.org/colleges/meredith-college.

14   "Academics," Winston-Salem State University, accessed August 16, 2015, https://www.wssu.edu/academics/.

15   "About," Christendom College, accessed August 16, 2015, http://www.christendom.edu/about/index.php.

Chapter 6: The Crisis of Standardlessness

1   "Table 322.10. Bachelor's Degrees Conferred by Postsecondary Institutions, By Field Of Study: Selected Years, 1970-71 Through 2013-14," in *National Center for Education Statistics*, accessed July 19, 2016, http://nces.ed.gov/programs/digest/d15/tables/dt15_322.10.asp.

2   Karen Herzog, "Scott Walker Announces GOP College Affordability Initiative," *Milwaukee-Wisconsin Journal Sentinel*, January 11, 2016, https://archive.jsonline.com/news/statepolitics/scott-walker-expected-to-announce-college-affordability-initiative-b99649359z1-364878671.html; Jessica Dickler, "Obama: We Have to Make College Affordable," *CNBC*, January 13, 2016, https://finance.yahoo.com/news/obama-college-affordable-130000717.html?guccounter=1&guce_referrer=aHR0cHM6Ly93d3cuZ29vZ2xlLmNvbS88&guce_referrer_sig=AQAAACTLAkpX-KF_VMo8NxkWUsy604SBljNJBjou7rnRqDBf5zus-iHCJi5sAuD7VZisAtGpdP0Fg7WvVqiY9xUJEa5v5ONWbLgkTZ8iD7SU2EWVqhaEKskWP9fLQp5UA4UM7uMYeStn1rghAI7Gu97FGZhhtFLysuuf94od2zJBoVct.

3   Glenn Colby, "Data Snapshot: Tenure and Contingency in US Higher Education," *American Association of University*

Professors, March 2023, https://www.aaup.org/sites/
default/files/AAUP%20Data%20Snapshot.pdf.

4 "Best National University Rankings," *U.S. News & World Report*,
accessed April 1, 2025, https://www.usnews.com/best-colleges/
rankings/national-universities?_sort=rank&_sortDirection=asc.

5 The hypothetical example just given about the anthropology
professors is just that: an imagined hypothetical case emanating
from the fertile depths of my imagination. The present author
actually conducted a series of tests using the real CVs of real
professors hired to real Assistant Professor jobs in various
fields of the humanities in 2008 to 2009 (not in the field of
anthropology, however). With the benefit of seven years of
hindsight, I compared the record of these scholars and found that
the scenario described hypothetically above has a firm basis in
reality. For reasons of discretion, obviously, I will neither mention
who the researchers are nor what discipline they practice.

6 The trend has been a long time coming. Marc Bousquet, a
trenchant and insightful critic of Higher Ed hypocrisy, noted
in 2003 that since 1968 "many departments have slowly
given up professorial lines." Marc Bousquet, "The Rhetoric
of 'Job Market' and the Reality of the Academic Labor
System," *College English* 66, no. 2 (November 2003): 220.

7 Steven Shulman, "Faculty and Graduate School Employment
at U.S. Colleges and Universities, 2013," Center for the
Study of Academic Labor, Department of Economics,
Colorado State University (January 2015): 1.

8 Marc Bousquet, "The Rhetoric of 'Job Market' and the Reality of
the Academic Labor System," *College English* 66, no. 2 (2003): 222.

9 Edward Ayers, "Where the Humanities Live," *Daedalus*
138, no. 1 (Winter 2009): 30; Franz Seifert, "I'd Go For
Collegiality Rather than Solidarity. The Social Sciences and
Humanities in a Crisis of Credibility on Top of all the Other
Crises," contribution to the workshop *Researching in Neoliberal
Conditions*, November 14–15, 2014, Vienna, Austria, 2.

10 Rebecca Schuman, "Why Your Cousin With a PhD is a Basket
Case: Understanding the Byzantine Hiring Process that Drives
Academics Up the Wall," *Slate*, September 23, 2014, http://www.
slate.com/articles/life/education/2014/09/how_do_professors_
get_hired_the_academic_job_search_explained.html.

Chapter 7: The Best College Teachers: Don't Believe the Hype

1   "*Literary Review*'s Bad Sex in Fiction Award," *Literary Review*, accessed August 5, 2016, https://literaryreview.co.uk/bad-sex-in-fiction-award.

2   Ken Bain, *What the Best College Teachers Do* (Harvard University Press, 2004), 4.

3   Ibid., 2.

4   Ibid., 111.

5   Ibid., 131.

6   Ibid., 19.

7   Rebekah Nathan, *My Freshman Year: What A Professor Learned by Becoming a Student* (Cornell University Press, 2005).

8   There are few scenarios more horrifying to a professor than living with students. Too, there are few scenarios more horrifying to an undercover researcher than to have some yutz figure out your identity. This came to pass when a journalist figured out that the author was Dr. Cathy Small who worked at Northern Arizona University. Diana Schemo, "What a Professor Learned as an Undercover Freshman," *The New York Times*, August 23, 2006, http://www.nytimes.com/2006/08/23/education/23FACE.html.

9   Rebekah Nathan, *My Freshman Year: What A Professor Learned by Becoming a Student* (Cornell University Press, 2005), 140.

10 Lindsey Burke, Jamie Hall, and Mary Reim, "Big Debt, Little Study: What Tax-Payers Should Know College Students' Time Use," *Issue Brief* no. 4589, July 19, 2016, http://www.heritage.org/research/reports/2016/07/big-debt-little-study-what-taxpayers-should-know-about-college-students-time-use.

11 Ibid., "Table 1: Many Full-Time College Students Put in Modest Hours," 3.

12 Alexander McCormick, "It's About Time: What to Make of Reported Declines in How Much College Students Study," *Liberal Education, American Association of Colleges and Universities* 97, no. 1 (Winter 2011), https://eric.ed.gov/?id=EJ936574.

13 Rebekah Nathan, *My Freshman Year: What A Professor Learned by Becoming a Student* (Cornell University Press, 2005), 8.

14 Ibid., 140.

15   Nathaniel Hawthorne, "The Minister's Black Veil," (1836) in
     The Celestial Railroad and Other Stories, (Signet Classics, 2006).
16   Georg Simmel, "The Stranger" (1908) in *On
     Individuality and Social Forms*, ed. Donald Levine
     (University of Chicago Press, 1971), 143–149.
17   Delbert Brodie, "Do Students Report that Easy Professors
     Are Excellent Teachers?" *The Canadian Journal of Higher
     Education* 28, no. 1 (1998): 1–20; Paul Isely and Harinder
     Singh, "Do Higher Grades Lead to Favorable Student
     Evaluations?" *The Journal of Economic Education* 36, no. 1
     (2005): 29–42; Andrew Ewing, "Estimating the Impact of
     Relative Expected Grade on Student Evaluations of Teachers,"
     Economics of Education Review 31 (2012): 141–154.
18   "Robert Foster Cherry Award for Great Teaching," *Baylor University*,
     accessed August 3, 2016, http://www.baylor.edu/cherry_awards/.
19   Daniel Chambliss and Christopher Takacs, *How College
     Works*, (Harvard University Press, 2014), 17–24.
20   Steven Shulman, *Faculty and Graduate Student Employment at
     U.S. Colleges and Universities, 2013*, Center for the Study of
     Academic Labor (Colorado State University, 2015): 1, https://
     csal.colostate.edu/docs/Employment-Report-2013.pdf

Chapter 8: Finding Your Good College Teacher: The Active Learning Approach

1   Aaron R. Hanlon, "My Students Need Trigger Warnings—and
     Professors do, too," *New Republic*, May 17, 2015, http://
     www.newrepublic.com/article/121820/my-students-need-
     trigger-warnings-and-professors-do-too; Matthew Beard, "I
     Triggered my Audience While Lecturing on PTSD. Here's
     What I Learned," *The Guardian*, July 14, 2015, http://www.
     theguardian.com/commentisfree/2015/jul/15/i-triggered-
     my-audience-while-lecturing-on-ptsd-heres-what-i-learned;
     Amanda Marcotte, "Trigger Warnings do Politicize Mental
     Illness. So What?" *Slate*, May 21, 2015, http://www.slate.com/
     blogs/xx_factor/2015/05/21/trigger_warnings_annoying_
     well_meaning_not_a_threat_to_free_speech.html.

2   *The Epic of Gilgamesh*, TAB III, (iv) 5–8, in *Ancient Near Eastern Texts Relating to the Old Testament with Supplement*, 3rd ed., ed. James B. Pritchard (Princeton University Press, 1969), 79.

3   Norbert Michel, John James Cater III, and Otmar Varela, "Active Versus Passive Teaching Styles: An Empirical Study of Student Learning Outcomes," *Human Resource Development Quarterly* 20, no. 4 (2009): 397.

4   Michael D. Shear and Tamar Lewin, "On Bus Tour, Obama Seeks to Shame Colleges into Easing Costs," *The New York Times*, August 22, 2013, http://www.nytimes.com/2013/08/23/us/politics/obama-vows-to-shame-colleges-into-keeping-costs-down.html.

5   Maxwell Tani, "Arizona Legislature Passes Deep Cuts to Public Universities," *The Huffington Post*, March 9, 2015, http://www.huffingtonpost.com/2015/03/08/arizona-education-cuts_n_6819886.html; Jordan Weissman, "A Truly Devastating Graph on State Higher Education Spending," *The Atlantic*, March 20, 2013, http://www.theatlantic.com/business/archive/2013/03/a-truly-devastating-graph-on-state-higher-education-spending/274199/.

6   Karen Herzog and Patrick Marley, "Scott Walker Budget Cut Sparks Sharp Debate on UW System," *Milwaukee-Wisconsin Journal Sentinel*, January 28, 2015, http://archive.jsonline.com/news/education/scott-walker-says-uw-faculty-should-teach-more-classes-do-more-work-b99434737z1-290087401.html.

7   Arthur Chickering and Zelda Gamson, "Seven Principles for Good Practice in Undergraduate Education," *AAHE Bulletin* 4 (1987); On the emergence of the method in the 1980s, see David Mello and Colleen Less, "Effectiveness of Active Learning in the Arts and Sciences," *Johnson & Wales University: Humanities Department Faculty Publications & Research*, Paper 45 (2013), http://scholarsarchive.jwu.edu/cgi/viewcontent.cgi?article=1044&context=humanities_fac.

8   John Drake, "A Critical Analysis of Active Learning and an Alternative Pedagogical Framework for Introductory Information Systems Courses," *Journal of Information Technology Education: Innovations in Practice* 11 (2012): 40.

9   Jennifer Faust and Donald Paulson, "Active Learning in the College Classroom," *Journal on Excellence in College Teaching* 9, no. 2 (1998): 4; David Mello and Colleen Less, "Effectiveness

of Active Learning in the Arts and Sciences," *Johnson & Wales University: Humanities Department Faculty Publications & Research*, Paper 45 (2013), http://scholarsarchive.jwu.edu/cgi/viewcontent.cgi?article=1044&context=humanities_fac.

10   Michael Prince, "Does Active Learning Work? A Review of the Research," *Journal of Engineering Education* 93, no. 3 (2004): 223.

11   Arthur W. Chickering and Zelda F. Gamson, "Seven Principles for Good Practice in Undergraduate Education," *AAHE Bulletin* 39, no. 7 (1987): 4.

12   Michael Prince, "Does Active Learning Work? A Review of the Research," *Journal of Engineering Education* 93, no. 3 (2004): 223–225.

13   Lakmal Abeysekera and Phillip Dawson, "Motivation and Cognitive Load in the Flipped Classroom: Definition, Rationale and a Call for Research," *Higher Education Research & Development* 34, no. 1 (2015): 3.

14   North Dakota State University College of Arts, Humanities, and Social Sciences, "Active Learning Activities," *NDSU*, accessed August 5, 2016, https://www.niu.edu/citl/resources/guides/active-learning-activities.shtml.

15   Norbert Michel, John James Cater III, and Otmar Varela, "Active Versus Passive Teaching Styles: An Empirical Study of Student Learning Outcomes," *Human Resource Development Quarterly* 20, no. 4 (2009): 399.

16   Jennifer Faust and Donald Paulson, "Active Learning in the College Classroom," *Journal on Excellence in College Teaching* 9, no. 2 (1998): 9.

17   Ibid., 17.

18   These prompts are taken from a lesson plan for Philip Roth's *American Pastoral* (Vintage Books, 1997), 360.

19   Scott Freeman et al., "Active Learning Increases Student Performance in Science, Engineering, and Mathematics," *PNAS* 111, no. 23 (2014); John Braxton et al., "The Role of Active Learning in College Student Persistence," *New Directions for Teaching and Learning*, no. 115 (2008): 80–81; Heidi Lujan and Stephen DiCarlo, "Too Much Teaching, Not Enough Learning: What is the Solution?" *Advanced Physiological Education* 30 (2006): 17; Craig Lambert, "Twilight

of the Lecture," *Harvard Magazine*, March 2012, http://
harvardmagazine.com/2012/03/twilight-of-the-lecture.

[20] David Mello and Colleen Less, "Effectiveness of Active
Learning in the Arts and Sciences," *Johnson & Wales University:
Humanities Department Faculty Publications & Research*,
Paper 45 (2013): 5, http://scholarsarchive.jwu.edu/cgi/
viewcontent.cgi?article=1044&context=humanities_fac.

[21] John Drake, "A Critical Analysis of Active Learning and an
Alternative Pedagogical Framework for Introductory Information
Systems Courses," *Journal of Information Technology Education:
Innovations in Practice* 11 (2012): 50; Norbert Michel, John James
Cater III, and Otmar Varela, "Active Versus Passive Teaching Styles:
An Empirical Study of Student Learning Outcomes," *Human
Resource Development Quarterly* 20, no. 4 (2009): 413–414.

[22] Elisa Park and Bo Keum Choi, "Transformation of
Classroom Spaces: Traditional Versus Active Learning
Classroom in Colleges," *The International Journal of Higher
Education Research* 68 (2014): 749, http://link.springer.
com/article/10.1007/s10734-014-9742-0/fulltext.html.

[23] Naturally, many in STEM disciplines are trying to configure
Active Learning techniques into large classes. I make no
judgments as to whether that will work in those fields. I
am adamant that it cannot work in the Humanities.

Chapter 9: Sex, Sloth, Subversion: The Professor's Daily Grind?

[1] This accusation is often made by conservative commentators. For
example, see Naomi Schaefer Riley, *The Faculty Lounges: And Other
Reasons Why You Won't Get the College Education You Pay For* (Ivan
R. Dee, 2011); Politicians make it as well. See Lucy McCalmont,
"Walker Urges Professors to Work Harder," *Politico*, January 29,
2015, http://www.politico.com/story/2015/01/scott-walker-
higher-education-university-professors-114716; Though one can
also detect this sentiment among non-conservative figures. See
Christopher Beam, "Finishing School: The Case for Getting Rid
of Tenure," *Slate*, August 11, 2010, http://www.slate.com/articles/
news_and_politics/politics/2010/08/finishing_school.html.

2   Philip Roth, *The Anatomy Lesson* (Vintage Books, 1983), 68.

3   Elaine Showalter, "Peeping Tom's Juvenile Jaunt," *The Chronicle Review*, November 12, 2004, http://www.chronicle.com/article/Peeping-Toms-Juvenile-Jaunt/17624.

4   Ibid.

5   Ibid.

6   Ibid.

7   Philip Roth, *My Life as a Man* (Vintage International, 1974), 230.

8   Ibid., 209.

9   Elaine Showalter, *Faculty Towers: The Academic Novel and its Discontents* (University of Pennsylvania Press, 2005), 100.

10 Ibid.

11 Elaine Showalter, "Peeping Tom's Juvenile Jaunt," *The Chronicle of Higher Education*, November 12, 2004, https://www.chronicle.com/article/peeping-toms-juvenile-jaunt/.

12 Billie Wright Dziech and Linda Weiner, *The Lecherous Professor: Sexual Harassment on Campus*, 2nd ed. (University of Illinois Press, 1990).

13 Josh Feldman, "O'Reilly To Stossel: Most College Profs Are Liberal We Need 'Affirmative Action For Conservative' Profs," *Mediaite*, December 4, 2012, http://www.mediaite.com/tv/oreilly-to-stossel-most-college-profs-are-liberal-we-need-affirmative-action-for-conservative-profs/; Jon Shields and Joshua Dunn Sr., *Passing on the Right: Conservative Professors in the Progressive University* (Oxford University Press, 2016), 193.

14 Neil Gross, *Why Are Professors Liberal and Why Do Conservatives Care?* (Harvard University Press, 2013), 7, 56; Scott Jaschik, "Moving Further to the Left," *Inside Higher Ed*, October 23, 2012, https://www.insidehighered.com/news/2012/10/24/survey-finds-professors-already-liberal-have-moved-further-left; Jon Shields and Joshua Dunn Sr., *Passing on the Right: Conservative Professors in the Progressive University* (Oxford University Press, 2016).

15 Neil Gross, "Table 1.1 Faculty Political Clusters by Type of Institution and Academic Field," in *Why Are Professors Liberal and Why Do Conservatives Care?* (Harvard University Press, 2013).

16 "About Us," *Heterodox Academy*, accessed October 31, 2016, http://heterodoxacademy.org/about-us/; Looking over the list of signatories, I am struck by how few in The Heterodox Academy are in the fields of literature, cinema studies, Women's

Studies and so forth. Of the 223 professors affiliated with the group, only 4 teach in English Departments, 1 in Art History, and none from Women's Studies or Cinema Studies.

17 Saeed Ahmad and Jacque Wilson, "UC Berkeley Student Group Votes to Disinvite Bill Maher; College Overturns it," *CNN*, October 30, 2014, http://www.cnn.com/2014/10/30/living/bill-maher-commencement-speaker/; Maher's equation of those protesting with liberals is evident in this clip from his show when he addresses the controversy over his commencement address at UC Berkeley. Bill Maher, "Bill Maher Responds to UC Berkeley Petition," *Real Time with Bill Maher*, October 31, 2014, https://www.youtube.com/watch?v=wcB-zvsRslY.

18 Janet Afary and Kevin B. Anderson, *Foucault and the Iranian Revolution: Gender and the Seductions of Islamism* (University of Chicago Press, 2005).

19 "Professor Calls for 'Million More Mogadishus,'" *CNN*, March 28, 2003, http://www.cnn.com/2003/US/Northeast/03/28/sprj.irq.professor.somalia/.

20 Ward Churchill, "'Some People Push Back': On the Justice of Roosting Chickens," *AK Press*, September 12, 2001.

21 Jacques Berlinerblau, "Introduction," in *Secularism on the Edge*, ed. Jacques Berlinerblau, Sarah Fainberg, and Aurora Nou (Palgrave Macmillan, 2014), 5.

22 Jon Shields and Joshua Dunn Sr., *Passing on the Right: Conservative Professors in the Progressive University* (Oxford University Press, 2016), 167.

23 Jon Shields and Joshua Dunn Sr., *Passing on the Right: Conservative Professors in the Progressive University* (Oxford University Press, 2016), 166–167.

24 Nancy Fraser, *Justice Interruptus: Critical Reflections on the "Postsocialist" Condition* (Routledge, 1997), 215.

Conclusion: The End: Cultivate Your Garden

1 Adam Davidson draws an analogy between exclusive nightclubs and elite schools. He argues that what makes the former similar to the latter is that both carefully curate who gets in. In this clever way of seeing things, it's the fabulous mix of people who makes a club/school special. Adam Davidson,

"Is College Tuition Really Too High?" *The New York Times*, September 8, 2015, http://www.nytimes.com/2015/09/13/magazine/is-college-tuition-too-high.html?_r=0.

2   Jacques Berlinerblau, "After Coronavirus, the Deluge," *The Chronicle of Higher Education*, March 26, 2020, https://www.chronicle.com/article/after-coronavirus-the-deluge/.

3   Jasper McChesney and Jacqueline Bichsel, *The Aging of Tenure-Track Faculty in Higher Education: Implications for Succession and Diversity*, College and University Professional Association for Human Resources (CUPA-HR), January 2020, https://www.cupahr.org/surveys/research-briefs/2020-aging-of-tenure-track-faculty-in-higher-ed-implications-for-succession-diversity/.

ACKNOWLEDGMENTS

The acknowledgments section of a scholar's book is yet another of those artless, endless, humble bragging, academic conventions that I could just as well do without. I'll keep it brief.

Throughout the writing of the first edition of this nonfictional campus novel from 2014 to 2016, I was assisted by Abra Burkett, Josh Shinbrot, Tiana Baheri, and Eitan Jay Sayag (who expertly dragged his old professor across the finish line). The second edition, or "glow up," was put together in early 2025 with the assistance of Jonathan Bar-On and Lainey Lyle.

Special thanks to my agent Michael Mungiello of Inkwell Agency who indulged my desire to have this reissued under my original title. All honor to the librarians everywhere who assist me, especially Jeffrey Popovich of Georgetown University.

This book is dedicated to my wife, finally. I salute my two sons, one still in college.

Like any professor my age, I've cumulatively taught a few thousand undergraduates across the arc of my career. To the kids (now parents, in many cases) at CUNY, Hofstra, and Georgetown: thank you. Thank you so much for letting me teach you and learn from you.

Washington DC
April 14th, 2025

ABOUT THE AUTHOR

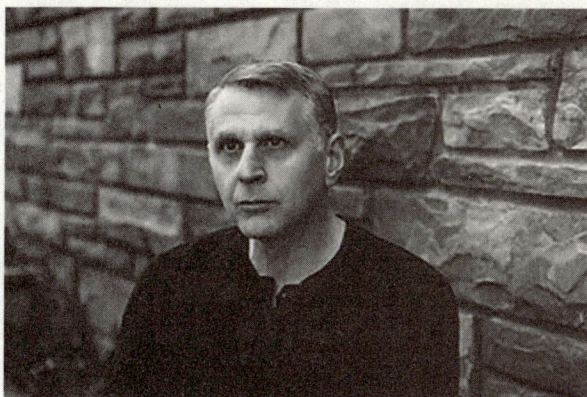

Image credit: David Baratz

Jacques Berlinerblau is a professor of Jewish Civilization at Georgetown University. He is also an op-ed writer for MSNBC and a scholar whose work has been discussed in fora ranging from *The New York Times* to *NPR* to the *Chronicle of Higher Education*. His work focuses on the interplay between culture and politics, and to this end, he has published twelve academic books and dozens of scholarly articles. His current research focuses on comedy that triggers massive cultural unrest.